Yiddish Poetry and the Tuberculosis Sanatorium

Judaic Traditions in Literature, Music, and Art
Harold Bloom *and* Ken Frieden, *Series Editors*

Other titles in Judaic Traditions in Literature, Music, and Art

American Hebrew Literature: Writing Jewish National Identity in the United States
Michael Weingrad

Classic Yiddish Stories of S. Y. Abramovitsh, Sholem Aleichem, and I. L. Peretz
Ken Frieden, ed.; Ken Frieden, Ted Gorelick, and Michael Wex, trans.

Early Yiddish Epic
Jerold C. Frakes, ed. and trans.

From Our Springtime: Literary Memoirs and Portraits of Yiddish New York
Reuben Iceland; Gerald Marcus, trans.

My Friendship with Martin Buber
Maurice Friedman

Place and Ideology in Contemporary Hebrew Literature
Karen Grumberg

Rhetoric and Nation: The Formation of Hebrew National Culture, 1880–1990
Shai P. Ginsburg

Who Will Die Last: Stories of Life in Israel
David Ehrlich; Ken Frieden, ed.

Yiddish Poetry and the Tuberculosis Sanatorium

1900–1970

Ernest B. Gilman

Syracuse University Press

Syracuse, New York 13244-5290

First Edition 2015
15 16 17 18 19 20 6 5 4 3 2 1

∞ The paper used in this publication meets the minimum requirements of the American National Standard for Information Sciences—Permanence of Paper for Printed Library Materials, ANSI Z39.48-1992.

For a listing of books published and distributed by Syracuse University Press, visit www.SyracuseUniversityPress.syr.edu.

ISBN: 978-0-8156-3379-2 (cloth) 978-0-8156-5306-6 (e-book)

Library of Congress Cataloging-in-Publication Data

Gilman, Ernest B., 1946– author.
Yiddish poetry and the tuberculosis sanatorium : 1900–1970 / Ernest B. Gilman. — First edition.
pages cm. — (Judaic traditions in literature, music, and art)
Includes bibliographical references and index.
ISBN 978-0-8156-3379-2 (cloth : alk. paper) — ISBN 978-0-8156-5306-6 (ebook)
1. Yiddish poetry—History and criticism. 2. Tuberculosis and literature. 3. Patients' writings—History and criticism. 4. Sanatoriums in literature. I. Title.
PJ5122.G55 2014
839'.11409—dc23 201402892

Manufactured in the United States of America

For the Iz and the Mo
and
In Memory of Jack Gilman

Ernest B. Gilman has taught at Columbia and the University of Virginia and is currently Professor of English at New York University. Specializing in Renaissance literature and in the literary history of medicine and disease, he has published numerous articles as well as four books of criticism in these areas, most recently *Plague Writing in Early Modern England* (University of Chicago Press, 2009).

Contents

Illustrations

Introduction

THE TUBERCULOSIS SANATORIUM was, in its day, a familiar feature of the American landscape. Its day began in 1882 when Edward Livingston Trudeau established the Adirondack Cottage Sanitarium—a therapeutic community, based on the European plan, that stressed the presumed benefits of clean air, ample nutrition, bed rest, and a post-Romantic belief "in the healing power of landscapes, the wilder and more 'natural' the better" (Caldwell 1988, 69).[1] Over the course of the nineteenth century, "consumption" had caused or contributed to more than one in five of all early deaths in the United States. By the 1880s, with the influx of mostly impoverished European immigrants densely packed into burgeoning eastern cities demographically ripe for the spread of infectious disease, the "white" plague loomed as the new-world counterpart to the "black plague" of earlier centuries. Into the 1950s and beyond, it would be no exaggeration to say that

1. See Caldwell, 57–71, on physicians Gustav Brehmer and his pupil Peter Dettweiler, the founders of the sanatorium model during the second half of the nineteenth century in Germany; and 53–159 on the "building boom" of "inns, pensions, and hotels" (153) in Davos, catering to the sort of leisured clientele familiar to readers of Mann's *The Magic Mountain*. To sort out a minor issue of terminology, Dormandy notes that the "sanatorium" and "sanitarium" (but sometimes also "sanitorium") were "often used interchangeably but their derivation is slightly different, the first from *sanare*, to cure, and the second from *sanitas*, health"—the one emphasizing "active medical intervention" and the other "healthy living" (1999, 147n1). Throughout, I follow the spelling adopted by the institutions themselves. For patients, who typically referred to the institution as the "san," it made no difference.

nearly every American knew someone—a family member, a friend, a neighbor—who was afflicted with tuberculosis. Adirondack Cottage, located in Saranac Lake, New York, and later renamed for its founder as the Trudeau Sanatorium, became the model for scores of like institutions, large and small, that sprang up across the country within the next twenty years in response to this crisis in the nation's health. The day of the sanatorium ended by the late 1950s, when tuberculosis was suddenly, and in many cases almost miraculously, "conquered" (as it then seemed) by Streptomycin and Isoniazid, the first-generation antibiotics in the physician's arsenal. Although these drugs and their variants had significant side effects, patients at death's door—some who had undergone brutal surgeries in a hapless attempt to arrest the disease—were virtually free of active tuberculosis just weeks after beginning the regimen.

By the end of the decade, nearly every one of the hundreds of sanatoriums in the United States had shut its doors. Many of their physical plants still stand, repurposed as hospitals and research facilities for other diseases, as geriatric centers, as schools, or—with a certain historical irony not lost on patients who experienced their time in the sanatorium as a form of incarceration—as prisons. The Cresson Tuberculosis Sanatorium in Pennsylvania, founded in 1916, became a mental hospital in 1956, and then reopened in 1987 as a state correctional facility.[2] The current owners of the former Waverly Hills Sanatorium in Kentucky are funding the restoration of the facility by offering "paranormal tours" (at $100 for the full night's experience) featuring the "Death Tunnel" once used "to transport the bodies of

2. Asylum Projects website, "Lawrence Frick State Hospital," http://www.asylumprojects.org/index.php?title=Lawrence_Frick_State_ Hospital (accessed March 22, 2013). A number of sanatoriums in the Adirondacks and the Catskills were transformed into prisons as well, providing an important source of income to residents in the area. The Ray Brook sanatorium, located between the towns of Saranac Lake and Lake Placid, now forms part of a federal prison facility (Caldwell 1988; 151, 270).

deceased TB patients" down the hill, and holding out the possibility of encountering the unquiet spirit of a dead lunger.[3]

Albeit by less paranormal means, my purpose in what follows is to recall the voices of the sanatorium—in particular, the voices of three notable tubercular Yiddish writers. I am not writing a history of TB, of the "search for the cure," or of the American sanatorium movement. In recent years these tasks have been undertaken by a number of historians and medical writers whose research has been motivated in large part by the realization that far from having been eradicated, tuberculosis has come back with a vengeance in MDR ("multi-drug resistant") and, worse, X-DR ("extensive drug-resistant") strains. In 2013 the World Health Organization registered its concern that treating patients with drugs to which they are resistant, a common practice in India, "can allow the bacteria to build resistance to new drugs as well" (Anand 2013, A1).[4] Thus renascent, tuberculosis adds to the dire catalog of afflictions once thought well controlled or virtually extinct—among the more alarming, lethal antibiotic-resistant staph infections that burn through hospital wards. The persistence of old, and the emergence of "new," diseases may well foreshadow a grim future, as climate change, famine, the rapid evolution and exchange of pathogens, and the seedbed

3. Waverly Hills Sanatorium website, http://www.therealwaverlyhills.com (accessed September 30, 2012). The *New York Times* reported in 2011 that a ghost-hunting reality show called "Paranormal Challenge" used Waverly Hills as the venue for one episode of the program (Genzlinger). Also among the stations of the cross for pilgrims in search of the paranormal, the Enos Sanatorium in Alton, Illinois, had earlier served as a safe house on the underground railroad. Presumably, one can sense the "lingering spirits of escaped slaves" communing with those of expired tuberculars: Alton Hauntings website, "Enos Sanatorium," http://www.altonhauntings.com/enos.html (accessed November 24, 2012).

4. The article focuses on Indian health policy ("morally and medically disastrous") and links this practice to a significant increase in MDR-TB cases in China, Russia, and parts of Europe as well as in India.

of a growing global population combine to engender the "coming plague."[5] My debt to this Cassandran literature, without which the present study would not have been possible, will be duly noted.[6]

Nor do I envisage a literary history of tuberculosis as it is conventionally written, from the top down—as a descent from high art to sentimental cliché. For readers of Keats, the poet's early death from the disease tinged his career with an aura of pathos and spiritual purification and helped to create the fashion for a consumptive pallor as evidence of a heightened sensibility. In retrospect it would be hard to resist finding the tubercular poet "half in love with easeful Death" in the "Ode to a Nightingale"—where "easeful death" rhymes with "quiet breath." Thoreau, who would succumb to tuberculosis at the age of forty-four, confided to his journal that "decay and disease are often beautiful, like the pearly tear of the shellfish and hectic glow of consumption" (Thoreau 1906, 92). When Kafka published his short story "A Hunger Artist" in 1922, two years before his death from the wasting sickness, the reflection of the consumptive writer in the *Hungerkűnstler* literally consumed by dedication to his art was both

5. I refer to the title of Laurie Garret's *The Coming Plague* (1994). Evidence for the near inevitability of a worldwide pandemic makes a sobering contribution to the new apocalypticism otherwise prefigured as a nuclear holocaust, a zombie invasion, or a religious rapture. Garret reports on a consensus among epidemiologists that in the near future such entirely predictable events as a laboratory accident or the sudden mutation of a pathogen will almost certainly produce a calamity like that of the "Spanish Flu" epidemic of 1918.

6. General sources recounting the medical history of the disease and advances in therapy in modern times begin with Dr. Gerald Webb's *Tuberculosis* (1936) and include Dr. Samuel Waksman's (prematurely titled) *The Conquest of Tuberculosis* (1964). Sources closer to my own historical and cultural interests in this book include Dormandy's *The White Death: A History of Tuberculosis* (1999), supplemented by Caldwell's *The Last Crusade* (1988) and Frank Ryan's *The Forgotten Plague* (1993) on the race for the cure, and Katherine Ott's *Fevered Lives* (1996). Sheila Rothman's *Living in the Shadow of Death* (1994) is a social history of the disease in America. On the JCRS, Jeanne Abrams's *Dr. Charles David Spivak* (2009) is the authoritative history.

clear and poignant. In Eugene O'Neill's *Long Day's Journey into Night* the tuberculosis of the younger brother Edmund darkens the tragedy of the Tyrone family. In these writers as well as in Chekhov, D. H. Lawrence, Robert Louis Stevenson, Stephen Crane, George Orwell, Alfred Jarry, and (too) many others, tubercular illness and art have been intimately connected. The critical narrative of tuberculosis seen from on high also encompasses healthy writers who created memorably afflicted characters. Alexandre Dumas's novel *The Lady of the Camellias* inspired the pathetic tubercular demise of Violetta at the end of Verdi's *La Traviata*. A character in one of Henri Murger's short stories was to become the Mimi of *La Boheme*. Most famously, of course, the sanatorium on Thomas Mann's *The Magic Mountain*, with its beautifully languishing residents, provides a symptom of Europe's malaise on the eve of the Great War.

Criticism from the top down might then trace the way tuberculosis as represented in these canonical authors is reproduced in the clichés of middlebrow and popular culture. Thus the demise of Beth in Louisa May Alcott's *Little Women* or, in our day, the death of Nicole Kidman's character Saline in the film *Moulin Rouge* owes nothing to clinical fact or to the lived experience of tuberculosis, but everything to the romantic tradition of the "transparent look" and the "indescribably pathetic beauty" in the face of the moribund patient (Alcott 1983, 456). William Cullen Bryant's 1824 "Sonnet to ——," written as his sister Sarah lay dying of consumption, addresses the victim: "Ay, thou art for the grave; thy glances shine / Too brightly to shine long." Death will take her as gently "As light winds wandering through groves of bloom / Detach the delicate blossom from the tree" (1854, 53). Such reveries allow us to imagine the moribund patients at Waverly fading into an incandescent ghostliness even before they crossed the threshold of the spirit world—rather than coughing out their last breath in the agony of suffocation, or choking on a sudden gush of hemorrhagic blood.

In this book I take the opposite approach by delving into the lived experience at the root of tubercular writing. Rather than tracing the formation of a tubercular imaginary infiltrated by the conventions of high art, I look at the relationships between the disease and the imagination from the ground up, describing the interplay of "high" and "low" from the perspective of the sanatorium, where the two converge at the scene of writing. My three principal writers were all sanatorium patients: Solomon Bloomgarten ("Yehoash"), Leivick Halpern ("H. Leivick"), and the Canadian poet and journalist Sholem Shtern are major figures in the history of twentieth-century Yiddish literature of the diaspora. Although each spent years as sanatorium patients, and each produced a significant body of work rooted in that experience, critical assessments of their careers and headnotes to anthologized selections of their poetry tend to mention this fact only in passing. In each case, my aim is to focus on these years as crucial to the writer's formation in the milieu of the tuberculosis sanatorium as an institution within which writing took place. Their work in and after the sanatorium emerges in turn from a larger body of writing—"lunger" lit, to appropriate a bit of "san" slang—produced by other patients and by their doctors, and preserved in the archives and publications of the sanatorium itself. These texts correlate the disease, the institution that produced them, and writing itself as a complex form of disclosure, consolation, immunization, and therapy. The broadest context for this project includes the theoretical and historical study of literature and medicine, disease and representation, and in particular the representation of the disease and the diseased as both subjects of, and subject to, the mores of the sanatorium, the central institution in the history of the white plague. For the sanatorium has its analogies to other institutional scenes of writing: prisons, military bases, mental institutions, perhaps even universities—all of which may be regarded as "clinical" in the broadest sense of Foucault's term.

Although my study ranges across the landscape of tuberculosis sanatoriums, I focus on two institutions in particular. Yehoash and, after him, Leivick, were patients in Denver's Jewish Consumptive Relief Society (the "JCRS")—in its day, from 1904 to 1954, one of the largest charitable sanatoriums in the western United States. Sholem Shtern, my third writer, was a patient in the Mount Sinai

Sanatorium in the Laurentian Mountains in Quebec. Situated on a scenic woodland tract, the Mount Sinai complex stood through the 1950s as "the jewel in the crown of Jewish philanthropy in Montreal" (Adams and Poutanen 2009, 1). In 1922 L. Meltzer, writing in *The Canadian Jewish Chronicle*, declared that "Of all the institutions Canadian Jewry has set up, there is not one, I venture to say, of greater importance than the Mount Sinai Sanatorium at Ste Agathe. For those suffering from the Great White Plague, it is a great blessing" (figure 1).[7]

The sanatorium is now demolished except for the abandoned ruin of the main building which can be explored by visitors equipped with a flashlight, a rope, and a "breathing mask" as protection against coal dust and moldering plaster contaminated with asbestos.[8] In Colorado, the JCRS was sufficiently populous to rate as its own town at the foot of the Rockies, named after the sanatorium's founder: Spivak, Colorado.[9] In the fifties, a part of its land was sold off to a shopping center developer. With the advent of the "cure," the JCRS was to have a happier fate than Mount Sinai. It first morphed into a cancer research center and now houses an art college. The small synagogue that served the spiritual needs of the lungers is currently being restored. The "pavilions" that housed generations of the afflicted still bear the names of the donor organizations that raised

7. "The Mount Sinai Sanatorium," January 13, 1922, 8.

8. These instructions for visiting Mount Sinai as an "Urban Exploration Resource" are posted at http://www.uer.ca/locations/show.asp?locid=20340 (accessed August 1, 2013). The visitor should also bring a metal detector to search for forgotten artifacts.

9. The JCRS treated more than ten thousand patients during its existence. In the twenties and thirties it housed as many as 250–300 patients at a time. The National Jewish Hospital across town on the east side of Denver had a somewhat larger capacity and also treated all patients free of charge. What distinguished the JCRS was its orthodox Jewish ambience, and even more, its willingness to admit patients in all stages of the disease, including those with very severe or terminal cases. Unlike a hospital, the JCRS, as a sanatorium with its own grounds, social facilities, and synagogue also formed the basis of a community.

1. The Mount Sinai Sanatorium in the Laurentian mountains of Quebec. Now a ruin, in Shtern's day, as pictured here, it was a burgeoning complex typical of other sanatoriums, with an imposing central building to which new housing facilities were added to accommodate a growing patient population. Photo courtesy of David and Elspeth Shtern.

the funds for their construction, and their cornerstones record the dates when, one after another, new facilities were put up to meet the needs of a growing patient population. I should stress that I do not offer the JCRS as a typical example of an American or indeed even of a Jewish-affiliated sanatorium. Across the country there were significant differences in local culture from one sanatorium to the next, differences depending partly on the size and location of the institution but also on the circumstances of its founding and, hence, on the makeup of its patient population. Some accepted only patients with mild or moderate infections. Others also admitted the terminally ill. Sanatoriums were founded for the wealthy and the destitute. They were established by churches, fraternal and labor organizations, individual physicians, and by state and municipal authorities.

2. The poet Leivick (right) seated next to Jack Gilman, on the grounds of the JCRS in Denver. Signed and inscribed on the back by the poet, "To my friend Gilman," and dated 1933. From Jack Gilman's photographs.

Nonetheless, the daily routine, the discipline of the cure, and the protocols of treatment were more or less standard everywhere (bed rest, diet, "heliotherapy," various surgical procedures designed to collapse a diseased lung in the hope that it would heal), and everywhere writing was encouraged as a therapeutic activity.

My reasons for focusing on the JCRS are both professional and personal—the latter, in that my father, Jack Gilman, took the cure at the JCRS in the thirties and was active in the literary circle surrounding Leivick, then a fellow patient (figure 2).

JCRS alumni and the physicians once affiliated with the sanatorium were very much part of my family's orbit as I was growing up in Denver in the 1950s. Indeed, as I was given to understand, after a generation of storekeepers and itinerant peddlers, recovered tubercular patients who chose to remain in Denver added significantly to the city's Jewish population during the half century of the sanatorium's operation. I began thinking about a project like this more than twenty years ago when I published a translation of Leivick's

"Ballad of Denver Sanatorium" in 1989 (discussed in chapter 3 and reprinted in appendix A), but four decades of teaching and writing about the literature of the English Renaissance had to be gotten out of the way first. Although some of my students imagine that I must have been born around the time of Shakespeare, this book is the first to draw on life as well as art. My last book, on *Plague Writing in Early Modern England* (2009), reawakened an interest in the literary history of epidemic disease and so proved to be the segue to the current project. The professional advantage for a study of Yehoash and Leivick in their lunger years is that a virtually complete set of JCRS records, including patient files, official correspondence, newsletters, and other publications, is preserved at the University of Denver under the auspices of the Rocky Mountain Jewish Historical Society. Along with the other original sources I have consulted, this archive, which has hardly been explored from a literary point of view, makes it possible to reconstruct the culture of the institution, of the lives lived, or lost, within its grounds, and of the creative work there fostered. Both Yehoash and Leivick recovered and returned to New York, but their writing was deeply influenced by life at the JCRS, as Shtern's was by Mount Sinai after his return to Montreal. While in residence, they contributed to the literary life of the institution, sharing their writing and inspiring other patients to take up the pen. My project thus addresses the "high" and the "low" registers of a therapeutic community's literary production. I analyze the poetry of Yehoash, Leivick, and Shtern as it engages and reflects upon their experience as institutionalized "lungers"; in turn, I analyze the body of amateur writing preserved in the archive, and the relations between the two. My aim in what follows is thus two-fold. First, I will look afresh at the work of my three tubercular Yiddish poets. In this respect this book makes its particular contribution to an understanding of the culture of Yiddish between 1900 and 1970 in the crucible of the tuberculosis sanatorium. Second, I understand their work as situated within, and growing out of, a larger body of tubercular writing produced by generations of mute, inglorious sanatorium patients and their doctors.

The themes of this literature, as I hope to show, are complex and intertwined. Nearly all the patients at the JCRS were of Orthodox Jewish background and born in Russia or Poland. Their exodus from Europe to a new home in—for the most part—New York was prolonged by a second exile, now to a sublime but (to them) utterly alien landscape two thousand miles distant, a place they could have only imagined beforehand from stories of the wild west that circulated even in eastern Europe.[10] Here, in the hope of recovery under the bright sun yet always under the shadow of death, they formed a new community. Theirs was a perilously liminal condition. Utopians under quarantine, refugees in the Promised Land but not of it, billeted on an ark or a plague ship, immune from persecution and the hardships that exacerbated their illness but under attack from a pathogenic enemy within. Observant by tradition, they were now compelled to ask, aloud or inwardly, why the God of Israel had cast them out. In these circumstances, the literature they produced engages the fundamental questions of dislocation and acculturation, life, death, tradition, and community. Among the most pressing issues addressed in this writing is the status of Yiddish, not only as a literary language but as the mark of what it means to be a Jew in an arena of competing cultural and political claims. Their writing functions as self-disclosure, communal voice, a form of therapy, and a form of denial. Their world, it might be argued, is distinctly a microcosm of the Jewish experience in America, *in extremis*. But their world in crucial respects also maps the sanatorium experience

10. In *Stardust Lost*, a study of Yiddish theater in America, Stefan Kanfer imagines the theater impresario Abraham Goldfaden pondering his decision to leave Bucharest in 1878: "Where to go? America?. . . . The papers spoke of a Lincoln County War in the territory of New Mexico. Somebody shot an Englishman, a friend of a crook called Billy the Kid. And then Billy put together a posse to kill the killers. It was crazy over there. Uncivilized. Wild" (2006, 23). As I discuss below, more than any other writer, the German Karl May (1842–1912) conjured up the European image of cowboys and Indians in a series of "western" novels translated into Yiddish, Hungarian, and Ukrainian among many other languages.

of other populations with whom they share a common citizenship in lungerland. The most comprehensive question prompting this study of three Yiddish tuberculars is, inevitably, what it means for an immigrant writer to be a Jew in America or in Canada in the first half of the twentieth century; and, as the more immediate question it subtends: how does the literature of the sanatorium define and respond to the issues of Jewish identity?

Chapter 1 delves into the archive of sanatorium publications in order to sketch the key features of the writing that appears in patient newsletters and in other extant documents of the Jewish sanatorium. Taken together, these materials allow us to reconstruct the sanatorium as an arena of literary production. The themes they reveal will establish the context for reading the work of the three professional writers discussed in the following chapters. Chapter 2 correlates the diverse projects undertaken by Yehoash during his years as a patient in, as well as a leading light in the establishment of, the JCRS sanatorium in the first decade of the twentieth century: a body of poetry, a Yiddish dictionary, a Yiddish translation of the Bible, and, oddly enough, a Yiddish translation of Longfellow's *Hiawatha*. Chapter 3 focuses on the poetry written by H. Leivick in the JCRS during the early 1930s, moving toward a reading of his most ambitious poem to come out of those years, the "Ballad of Denver Sanatorium." Chapter 4, on the Canadian Yiddish poet Sholem Shtern, opens a longer historical perspective. Shtern's verse novel *The White House*, based on the author's stay at the Mount Sinai Sanatorium outside Montreal in the late 1920s, was written forty years later, after the Holocaust. The novel's concern with the relations between its Jewish lungers and the French Canadian farmers in the same area of the Laurentian mountains as Mount Sinai refracts the question of Canadian Jewish identity as much in light of the Québécois separatist movement of the 1960s as in that of the legacy of Yiddish cultural politics in the 1920s and beyond.

Acknowledgments are due to the Memorial Foundation for Jewish Culture for their support of the research that led to this book, and to the Abraham and Rebecca Stein Faculty Publication Fund for assistance with publication. Dr. Jeanne Abrams and Thyria Wilson were invaluable as my guides to the JCRS materials in the Beck Archives of Rocky Mountain Jewish History, Special Collections, at the Penrose Library of the University of Denver. Thanks as well to the congenial reference staff at the libraries of the University of Colorado at Colorado Springs, the Denver Public Library, and the Colorado Springs Public Library. For all matters Yiddish, the YIVO library in New York is a vast treasure house which the keepers of the keys are dedicated to sharing with scholars working there. Florence Mulhern kindly spent time with me in discussion of her novel *The Last Lamb on the Mountain*. David Shtern was most congenial in our discussions of his father Sholem's experience at the Mount Sinai Sanatorium. I am grateful for his comments as well as for his willingness to share family photos with me and to give permission for me to reprint them and to quote material from his father's verse novel *The White House*. Jennika Baines and her colleagues at Syracuse University Press were as long-suffering with me as they were professional in shepherding my book into print. A special note of thanks goes to Sunny Yudkoff, to my research assistants Michael Fleishman and Elizabeth Crawford, and to NYU undergraduates Sedera Ranaivoarinosy and Ingrid Bengtsson.

A Note on Translation: All translations from the Yiddish are my own unless otherwise noted; where individual poems have been published in translation I have preferred to use them. As the Hebrew alphabet will be Greek to many readers, I do not use it to represent Yiddish words. Nor, with rare exceptions where the sound or other nuance of the word is important, do I employ the conventional phonetic transcription of Yiddish (e.g., "verterbukh" for dictionary), as these usages will mean nothing to those who know no Yiddish, and will be pointless to those who do. Little is to be gained by transliterating the name *Henri Vadzvorth Longfello* from the title page of Yehoash's *Hayavata*, although I cite Yehoash's title in referring to his translation rather than to Longfellow's original poem. My own translations are intended to be as literal as possible, cleaving to the form and vocabulary of the Yiddish original, and with as little collateral damage as possible to English sense and word order. Any literary merit in my translations is to be attributed to serendipity alone. My translation of H. Leivick's "Ballad of Denver Sanatorium" was originally published in the *Rocky Mountain Jewish Historical Notes* (Summer/Fall 1989), 3–9, and is reprinted by permission in appendix A.

Yiddish Poetry and the Tuberculosis Sanatorium

1

The Poetics of Lunger Lit

The Hidden Spark

Nearly every tuberculosis sanatorium in America sponsored a newsletter or magazine to which patients and members of staff contributed poems, essays, letters, anecdotes, gossip, reminiscences, book reviews, comic pieces and jokes, plays, notices of current events, and medical advice. These publications were normally edited by patients; others of a more official nature were produced by the sanatoriums themselves. Wherever archives of these documents have been preserved, they offer a detailed account of the institution's ethos and of the residents' daily lives. More than a way of filling idle hours of bed rest or "heliotherapy," reading and writing were regarded as an important means to the cure. Offering a substantial trove of "amateur" material, these newsletters provide the context for understanding the work of the "professional" writers explored in the chapters that follow. The main body of material for this chapter comes from the publications of the JCRS—the Denver sanatorium where Yehoash and Leivick chased the cure. Writings by patients and doctors in other institutions—including the Trudeau Sanatorium in Saranac Lake, the National Jewish Hospital in Denver, the Glockner Sanatorium and the Cragmor Sanatorium, both in Colorado Springs—will also be taken into view. In some cases the differences between these sanatoriums were sharp, as between the JCRS, a charity institution serving mostly indigent Jews who could hardly afford the train fare to Denver, and Cragmor in Colorado Springs, which catered to the needs of wealthy Christians. A penniless button-hole maker in the

JCRS lived in a very different world from that of "Mr. McCue and Mister Lampton" who, as reported in the Cragmor newsletter, "have left on a motor trip through Yellowstone Park," Mr. Lampton having "purchased a new Buick" for the occasion (*Ninety Eight.Six* [*NES*] 32.4 [1928]).[1] But the rich and the poor in Colorado or, like Sholem Shtern in rural Quebec, shared a landscape of mountains, sunlight, and snow. Institutionalized "lungers" everywhere lived under the shadow of death made all too visible on the X-ray plate. The fundamental regimen of the cure—sunlight, rest, ample food, artificial pneumothorax and other more drastic surgical procedures, rigid rules of conduct (and the means of evading them)—as well as the patients' experience of sanatorium life are remarkably similar across differences in the size, location, or religious connection of the facility.[2] So, too, was an emphasis on reading and writing.

The therapeutic value of literature as part of the sanatorium regimen had its influential professional advocates. Dr. Gerald B. Webb, president of the National Tuberculosis Association (1920–1921) and founder of the Colorado Foundation for Research in Tuberculosis (1924), argued at length for the efficacy of literature in the

1. More from the elite Cragmor Sanatorium's newsletter *Ninety Eight.Six*: "Mr. Ostendorf wishes to announce that he was not caught when the bottom fell out of the market"; he had a tip "and sold his entire stock at a profit of nearly twenty-five percent" (*NES* 4.1 [1924], 8). Between 1895 and 1915, in addition to any number of boarding houses renting rooms to tuberculosis patients, at least a dozen sanatoriums were established in the Denver–Colorado Springs area, including the Catholic Montcalme Sanatorium specializing in the water cure ("walking on dew-fresh grass and snow"), the Colored Preachers Home, the Union Printers Home, and the Battle Creek Sanatorium for those following the health regimen of Dr. John Harvey Kellogg (vegetarian diet and "electric" baths). See Hoff and Gilfillan-Morton (2005), 21–22, 35.

2. As a question of method, I note that the examples of patient writing in this chapter are organized thematically rather than chronologically or by sanatorium. Similar entries (on the sanatorium's resemblance to a monastery, for instance) appearing ten years apart are in fact similar because the structure and culture of the institution remained virtually unchanged over the half-century of its existence.

treatment of the disease.[3] Webb's essay "The Role of the Physician in Literature" assembles an impressive catalog of writers (among them Rabelais, Thomas Lodge, Sir Thomas Browne, John Locke, and Oliver Goldsmith) who also practiced medicine and for whom, Webb believed, the two vocations of author and doctor were closely allied (*NES* 37.1 [1929], 8–10). In 1930 he followed up with a substantial essay in the *Journal of the American Clinical and Climatological Association* entitled "The Prescription of Literature."[4] Returning to his list of literary physicians, Webb finds evidence that Rabelais "prescribed literature" to his patients and reminds us that in the French author's "immortal book we learn that Gargantua, suffering from insomnia, was put to sleep by a reading of the Psalms!" (1930, 263). No less pertinent than bizarre as an example of medical intervention in the interest of self-expression was Rabelais's invention "of a surgical instrument [the glottotome] wherewith he cut the tongue of an inarticulate woman," presumably allowing her to regain her voice (263). Insofar as literature can refresh the mind and help us forget our misfortunes, Webb concludes that "there are many times when it is incumbent on the wise physician to prescribe, not a posset or a purgative, but an essay or a poem" (262). One book Webb particularly recommends is *The Poetry Cure: A Pocket Medicine Chest of Verse* (Schauffler 1925), an anthology divided into groups of poems suitable for different afflictions (274).

"But perhaps it is too much to expect the sick room to turn into a college of liberal arts," Webb concedes. "Even if this is so, the ultimate cultural value of sick bed reading is for us secondary to its immediate curative effect" (267). Knowing which books to prescribe

3. The foundation became the Webb-Waring Institute in 1926 when Webb—who had emigrated from England to find a cure for his wife's tuberculosis and devoted himself after her death to tuberculosis research—was joined by Dr. James J. Waring, Webb's patient. The institute was originally located in Colorado Springs at Colorado College.

4. Webb's essay is excerpted in Cragmor's *Ninety Eight.Six* (48.4 [1931], 1–3) and in the publications of other sanatoriums.

requires an assessment of the patient's temperament. "The mind, like the body, will thrive best on a mixed diet" and so requires "the variety of a number of literary forms" for the proper nutrition (278). Books, like medications and nourishment, must be administered according to the patient's condition and temperament:

> Aristotle, the founder of literary criticism, went to some length to explain the effect of high tragedy; but we cannot be sure that the purging of the passions which he describes will be the result of tragedy on all members of the audience. Some men—especially those with a fine feeling for the struggle of the drama—will be exhilarated by a reading of *Jude the Obscure*; others will most certainly be depressed by this spectacle of man being overwhelmed by fate. Indeed, I suspect that there are many who might read Hardy with no ill effects when well, who would find him too gloomy when read in a sick bed. Perhaps for most persons it would be safer to prescribe Dickens than Hardy, Galsworthy than Dreiser, Thomas Mann than Arnold Zweig. (268)

As if filling Webb's prescription, the Cragmor's *Ninety Eight. Six*, along with other sanatorium publications in which his work appeared, regularly featured book reviews and literary articles. Whether reprinted from other sources or more frequently written by patients themselves, essays appeared in *Ninety Eight.Six* on Hardy, Hemingway, Marx, Joyce's *Ulysses*, Defoe's *Journal of the Plague Year*, and Eugene O'Neill; and in the JCRS newsletters, on Herzl, Sholem Aleichem, and Yiddish poetry.[5] As a patient at the JCRS (and the Chair of the Press and Propaganda Committee), Yehoash lent his

5. The JCRS's *Hatikvah* 6.8 (1930) is typical in including a section of book reviews, in this issue, on *A Farewell to Arms*, Trotsky's autobiography, and the *Confessions of Zeno* by Italo Svevo (16–17), as well as an article on the growth of Yiddish as a literary language and a "living form of expression" (19). The books reviewed in this issue were added to a growing collection donated to the sanatorium library. *Tales of the Tents*, an early JCRS newsletter, advises "a daily schedule of instructive reading, suited to individual tastes and requirements" (January 1918, 3).

support to *The Sanatorium*, the institution's first newsletter, contributing two poems to its 1907 inaugural issue, "Der Sterbender Konsomptiv" (The Dying Consumptive) and, in English, "The White Plague" (1.1 [1907], 11, 30).[6]

As part of their therapy, tubercular patients were encouraged to write as well as to read. To be sure, serious patients consigned to complete bed rest might be prohibited from doing either, for fear that the excitement would fuel their fever and worsen their condition. Rather than purging the passions, reading the wrong sort of book might even inflame them—a concern that harks back to the earliest criticism of the novel, from which we learn "languishing and affectedly sentimental compositions . . . tend to give the mind a degree of weakness, which renders it unable to resist the slightest impulse of libidinous passion" (Knox 1778). If words on the page could affect the body as deeply as Dr. Webb believed, then it was only prudent to guard against a literary overdose. Prompted nonetheless by the urging of such a renowned tuberculosis specialist, sanatorium newsletters all solicited contributions from their readers, occasionally by sponsoring literary contests with modest cash prizes for the best poems and short stories submitted for publication. In an article entitled "Literary and Dramatic Activities of Patients," the editors of *Hatikvah* were eager to motivate their fellow residents of the JCRS to take up their pens in the belief that the journal "could be made, with comparatively little effort on your part, a most potent force in Sanatorium life, and a valuable factor in the cure and prevention of

6. In 1912 *The Sanatorium* reprinted in translation a Yehoash story that originally appeared in the Yiddish press in New York. "And Both Were Waiting" features two Colorado lungers at death's door, both eager to get back to New York to die in the bosom of their kin but too poor to afford the train fare. They then learn that when a corpse is shipped back east by train a living passenger must accompany the casket—for free, since his fare is paid by the grieving family. The two paupers naturally develop a keen curiosity in each other's health (or lack thereof). "And thus they sat, day in and day out, and carried on their silent competition" to see "who would die last" (6 [1912], 1–6).

tuberculosis." So you "think you have no writing ability? Make an attempt; you have time, and, even while in bed, dreaming and hoping, share your dreams and woes with your fellow patients! Woes and grief? 'Unload' by writing for *Hatikvah*" (4.3 [1926], 9). *PEP*, the magazine of the Firland Sanatorium in Washington state, sponsored its literary contest in the belief that "With its contemporaries, *PEP* plays an important part in the never ceasing battle against tuberculosis" (August [1937], 10). The announcement of a similar competition in the National Jewish Hospital's *Fluoroscope* featured "a short lesson in poetry writing" intended to "kindle that hidden spark in your inner self and after trying it for fifteen minutes a day you will come to the astounding realization that you are, after all, a budding poet" (1.9 [1930], 3).

The conviction that lungers could, and should, write poetry and fiction as a form of therapy was based on assumptions very different from those that lay behind the relation between consumption and creativity in the romantic imagination. In literary precincts outside the sanatorium, it might be imagined that the creative flame burned all the brighter in the feverish, nearly transparent, less fleshly and therefore somehow more spiritualized body of the terminal consumptive. The stronger the intimations of mortality, the better the poetry. The voice that spoke through a purified body already more dead than alive seemed to come from beyond the grave. Arguably, the consumptive artist in this fantasy might, if she were asked, be more than willing to trade her inspiration for the ability to breathe without coughing up gobbets of blood and ultimately drowning in her own pulmonary fluids. Within the sanatorium, as part of an institutional regime emphasizing hopefulness and the patient's "morale resisting power" as much as his "physical resisting power" ("each counting 50%," according to prominent Denver physician Arthur Rest), the prescription of literature could help alleviate "pathogenic pessimism" (JCRS *Ear-Bender* [*EB*] 1.3 [1940], 6). Patients were warned on the basis of sound medical authority that "Anxiety and worry supply ample nourishment for the tubercle bacilli" (*Fluoroscope* [*F*]

2.6 [1930], 4). If the "poisons of fear are added to the toxins of tuberculosis," the patient "makes no progress" (*PEP*, July [1938], 18). In the absence of any magic bullet, writing, as a means of alleviating fear and boosting morale, was served along with diet, bed rest, and sunlight as a means of detoxifying the tubercular body.

On the evidence, few among the budding poets in America's tuberculosis sanatoriums flourished in their literary pursuits. The professional writer Betty MacDonald—whose experience as a patient at Firland provided the material for her popular memoir *The Plague and I* (1948)—was recruited as an associate editor of *PEP* during her stay in the sanatorium (1938–1939) because she could type. When she raised questions about the woeful quality of the manuscripts put before her, she was told she could not change a word, even to correct the grammar, presumably because to do so would edit out the patient's true feelings (MacDonald 1948, 220). In *The Last Crusade*, a history of the war on consumption, Mark Caldwell characterizes these newsletter effusions as "Doggerel verse and giddy inspiration pieces pour[ing] forth from the invalids," and always accepted so long as "they seemed spontaneous, fostered camaraderie, toed the optimistic line, and avoided the appearance of professionalism" (1988, 106). This is at best a partial judgment, as the examples of patient writing adduced below will confirm. *Fluoroscope*'s January 1930 "short lesson in poetry writing" would, however, seem to warrant Caldwell's easy condescension. From our instructor Bela J. Rosenfield we learn that for poetry "rhyme is the most important thing, and love the most splendid subject." Or if not in love, we may find that "hidden spark" by looking out the window, for "Nothing equals our glorious West in natural beauty." The winners of the contest were announced the following month in the February 1930 issue of *Fluoroscope* (1.10, 2–6). One prize was awarded to Yoshio Shitamae for his entry "Opportunity Comes But Once" (urging patients to take advantage of the training available at the NJH vocational school), while Edward Custer earned an Honorable Mention for "Do We Want Quiet?" (an appeal to cut down the noise level in the hospital). First prize went to Mabel Glaesel, who takes Bela's advice to heart in her winning poem, "Lift Thine Eyes to the Mountains."[7]

If much sanatorium writing was relentlessly upbeat, then one rejoinder might be that of a wag writing in the newsletter of the Cragmor Sanatorium: if patients were to write about the more brutal realities of sanatorium life, who would be moved by a literature "filled with hemorrhages, temp sticks, X-rays and pneumothorax," or "enthralled by the crisis of phrenicectomy or thoracoplasty?" (*NES* 49.1 [1935]). A more considered response would understand how even the flimsiest constructions of ersatz cheerfulness stood on the solid bedrock of despair. If the archive of sanatorium newsletters is amply supplied with poetical exhortations on hope, faith, patience, and the benefits of a positive attitude, the salt to balance these artificial sweeteners of institutional life is to be found in the joke sections usually printed near the poetry:

> 1ST PATIENT—"What book are you reading?"
> 2ND PATIENT—"Last Days of Pompeii."
> 1ST PATIENT—"What did he die of?"
> 2ND PATIENT—"An eruption." (*PEP*, December [1938], 15)

> SADIE: "Lived here all your life?"
> EVA: "Don't know, haven't died yet." (*Hatikvah* [*H*], April [1927], 13)

> "Boys, I'm being cured"
> "Yeh: So is ham!" (*H*, April [1930], 19)

> "Some day, infallibly, I shall die and leave you."
> "How much?" (*H*, May [1927], 11)

During World War I, the JCRS *Tales of the Tents* published a complaint by the "poor little helpless" tubercle bacillus speaking on

7. The final stanza: "Lift thine eyes to the mountains, / There is strength in the mountains, / God illumines the mountains / With heavenly fire!"

behalf of his fellow germ(an)s, who find themselves assaulted by sunlight and antiseptics. "You know we little germans have no organization, no leadership, no efficiency, no Kultur. When we get into a lung, what's a little shortness of breath compared to being gassed?" (*Tales of the Tents*, June [1918], 1).[8] Jokes and "doggerel" notwithstanding, the archive also features a good many patient contributors of non-negligible literary ability as well as of considerable critical interest. They offer moments of insight into the realities and fantasies that, altogether, frame the image of sanatorium life as lived on the inside, as well as of the writers' work to be discussed in the chapters that follow.

The New Eden

When H. Leivick published *Lider fun Gan Edyn*, the collection of poems written during his years at the JCRS, the title evoked an Edenic image of Colorado as old as the westward movement. These were Leivick's "Poems from Paradise," or more literally, in the Yiddish, "Poems from the Garden of Eden." Leivick's tubercular "Gan Edyn" is tinged with irony—but even so, his work draws on, and plays against, a long history of Edenic allure. As much as by gold strikes and homesteading, easterners were drawn to God's country for its salubrious climate, their trek facilitated after 1870 by the extension of the railroad to Denver. In 1895, Dr. Edwin Solly, one of the founders of the Cragmor Sanatorium, published *The Health Resorts of Colorado Springs and Manitou*, a pamphlet extoling the virtues of the climate as part of a campaign orchestrated by local

8. In World War II as well, sanatorium writing linked the fight for the cure—the last "crusade," as Caldwell sees it, evoking the militant spirit of the March of Dimes and the National Tuberculosis Association—to the fight against fascism. Thus, Otto Langer, writing in the NJH *Fluoroscope* in 1943, sees the fight for the recovery of our health as "part of the bigger fight, the fight of the preservation of the ideals for which the United States stands ("The Future and Us," 14.1, 7–8). The two "fights" were more directly linked insofar as soldiers and potential draftees were afflicted by tuberculosis.

railroad baron and entrepreneur William Palmer to boost the population of the town (Rothman 1994, 150–51). For such a claim there was convincing medical evidence. In 1850, celebrated physician Dr. Daniel Drake reached the conclusion, based on his study of "medical topography," that the right regional conditions "may be presumed to exercise an influence either directly or indirectly on health" (Drake 1850, Preface). In the JCRS *Hatikvah*, the author of "Colorado Sketches" describes the therapeutic influence of the landscape: "the rich red-brown of the mountains, the occasional patches of snow, the crystal clarity of that atmospheric blue sky." The effects of these natural wonders on the patient's literary ambition are described as something between a seduction and a psychotherapy session: "So, even we succumb to the beauty of Colorado, little that we see from our windows, and finally, but as yet reluctantly, disclose our innermost response to it" (April [1930], 3).

Compared with the pestiferous cities of the eastern seaboard, any rural sanatorium might boast such a benevolent influence from its location alone. Drake, however, argued that the "voiceless solitudes of the desert" were ideally suited to the purpose (Drake 1850, Preface). As evidence of such a claim, in 1860 another physician reported—quite wrongly—that among the Native Americans in the region "tubercular consumption is almost unknown" (135). Rothman cites the popular travel writer Bayard Taylor, who proclaimed in 1867 that "Colorado will soon be recognized as our Switzerland" (Taylor 1867, 166). The advent of the sanatorium would prove him right. Why chase the cure all the way to Davos, even if (as was the case only of patients in elite private sanatoriums) one could afford the passage? In 1884 the English travel writer Iza Harry judged Colorado Springs to be "a veritable Eden for consumptive invalids" (Harry 1881, 101). As a result of its presumed therapeutic advantages tirelessly promoted in publicity campaigns like Palmer's, by 1900, Rothman estimates, fully "one third of the newcomers to Colorado had come in search of health" (132). A pamphlet published by Denver's Swedish Consumptive Sanatorium around 1905 touts Colorado as "the land of eternal sunshine, the Switzerland of America."[9] In 1930 the JCRS newsletter *Hatikvah* imagines the enthusiasm of a first-time visitor who, knowingly or not, echoes what had by then become a commonplace reaction: "The sanatorium looks like the Garden of Eden. How easy one breathes out here among the fragrance of the flowers and blooming trees" ("A Layman Looks Around," 6.7, 1–2, 9). In such a setting—as much constructed by art as provided by nature—even the lunger near death could dare to imagine the sanatorium as the womb of a new birth, even if skeptically: "Three months was the gestation period at The Pines. We were conceived in the Administration Building, confirmed by a staff doctor, approved by a Charge Nurse and for the next three months existed as embryos carefully fed and cared for by the Mother Hospital, alive but not living" (MacDonald 1948, 176).

For Jewish lungers in Colorado, the moment when life is breathed into the first humans in *Gan Eydn* stands at the origin of the Torah's narrative of exile, wandering, captivity, exodus, and finally, once the hardships of the desert have been endured, the prospect of a Promised Land. The Passover 1930 issue of the NJH *Fluoroscope* grimly reminds its readers that they are suffering from a "tyrant disease" worse than Pharaoh himself. But the celebration of the exodus should encourage the lungers at the Seder table to think of themselves as the children of Israel suffering sorrow and pain in order "to purify their souls" in the "sands of the desert, under free skies." Sick as they may be, they should be confident that they are "on the threshold of a land flowing with milk and honey." Passover teaches us not to let "our broken bodies enslave our spirits." Here, in Colorado-on-the-Sinai, we no longer breathe the "contaminated, foul air of Egypt" (1.12, 5).

The following year the same magazine reprinted "Seder in a Promised Land," an earlier article by a writer who "had been a bed

9. Denver Public Library, Western History/Genealogy Dept.: Swedish Medical Center records.

patient for nine months and had never been in the dining room." Now released from his bondage to the bed and able to partake of the celebration, he is heard to exclaim that he knew "[t]he West would be my promised land" (*News of the National*, October [1931], 6–7). Dr. Drake, the medical topographer, urged the infirm to "pitch their tents" in the desert "and plunge into rustication" (Drake 1850, 175). As it happens, the earliest patients in the JCRS and other sanatoriums in the Rockies lived in tents. The temporary wooden cabins into which they were subsequently moved to await construction of more permanent facilities still went by that name, and the earliest of the JCRS sanatorium publications was called *Tales of the Tents*. The rabbis had long understood the tents in which the Israelites lived during their forty years in the desert as a symbol of the synagogue. The latter-day Israelites of the JCRS, virtually all of them with orthodox, Eastern European roots, would have known by heart the Hebrew prayer *Ma Tovu* recited by the faithful every morning upon entering the synagogue for the *shacharit* service, and beginning with the verse from Numbers 24:5, "How goodly are thy tents, O Jacob, and thy tabernacles, O Israel!" For patients in this frame of mind, the sanatorium symbolized a return to the future: at once a destination and, God willing, a new beginning.

The Living Dead

The west, however, was a Promised Land in which the promise—of healing, of returning to home and family—might or might not be fulfilled. The bright optimism of sanatorium publications everywhere was often shaded by humor or irony, but seldom darkened by any mention of death. Patients known (by everyone) to have died were often listed in the newsletters as "departed," "outgoing," or "discharged." Their remains were typically spirited out by night through corridors or tunnels whose existence for this purpose was never mentioned. Suicides were not unheard of. "I seen 'em come and I seen 'em go," an orderly at the "Pines" confides to patient Betty Macdonald: "Some go out on their feet but most of 'em go out in a box" (1948, 67). The poet Adelaide Crapsey, best known for her elegy on Keats, preferred to convalesce (and, in 1914, to die at the age of 36) in a private boarding house in Saranac Lake rather than in Trudeau's nearby sanatorium. From her window she could clearly see what the sanatorium patients could not: the graveyard in which the "departed" lungers were laid to rest. "To the Dead in the Graveyard Underneath my Window," written in a "Moment of Exasperation," cries out to the dead:

> Oh, have you no rebellion in your bones!
> The very worms must scorn you where you lie,
> A pallid, mouldering, acquiescent folk,
> Meek inhabitants of unresented graves.
> Why are you there in your straight row on row
> Where I must ever see you from my bed
> That in your mere dumb presence iterate
> The text so weary in my ears: "Lie still
> And rest; be patient and lie still and rest."
> I'll not be patient! (1915, 75, ll.8–17)

The poet who says in her letters that she writes "with a very cold and stiff hand" and that consumption can "make you feel perfectly dead" (1977, 245, 238) imagines the "inhabitants" of the graveyard still as the obedient sanatorium patients they once were. From Crapsey's point of view, the prime directives of the cure—"be patient," "lie still and rest"—have become stage directions for playing dead in earnest when the time comes.

The mortality rate across the landscape of American sanatoriums is estimated at one in three, and very likely higher at institutions like the JCRS that accepted patients with advanced cases of the disease.[10] The sanatorium was hailed as the vanguard in the fight for the cure,

10. For the year 1912, Denver's Swedish Sanatorium noted in its annual report that of 72 patients treated—6 with stage 1, 21 with stage 2, and 47 with stage 3—14 stage-3 patients died and 24 had not yet improved. Treatment centered on heliotherapy and cold baths. The following year, 1913, would herald a new regimen of "immunized goat serum and an inhalation treatment of nitrous oxide, ethanol iodide, and creosote" (Hunt 2005, 20).

and yet there is no hard evidence that rates of survival were lower or higher among the majority of American tuberculosis victims who sought private treatment, who put their faith in quack cures, or who availed themselves of no treatment at all. One historian takes the extreme view that sanatoriums "were ineffective, and perhaps even unnecessary," arguing that their success as an institution stemmed alike from the psychological comfort they offered to the afflicted and from the interest of the state in isolating the contagious in "a modern and humane version of the pesthouse" (Ott 1996, 150–51).

Given the power of official disavowal—the refusal to see, or let others see, what lies before one's eyes—it is all the more remarkable to find those moments in the sanatorium archive when the scales drop away and a patient records what he *doesn't* see, as in the final stanza in the English poem called "My Wall" by National Jewish Hospital patient J. W. Taff (*F* 14.3 [1943]):

> Nothing, nothing,
> At all is written
> On my wall
> Of the many who have gone before
> No single sign
> No explanatory line
> Of how they went —— by what door
> No, there is no solitary trace
> Of the many eyes
> That have for one last time
> Grasped at this silent face
> And then forever fell
> From time and place
> No, nothing at all
> Is there
> But vacant space ——

In a Yiddish poem entitled "Chained" and published in *Hatikvah* in 1923, Abraham Druskin cannot tear his eyes from the "bewitching mountains." Though "free," he lies "in bed a captive." Thus held down, he stretches out his arms to the Rockies hoping to feel a cool breath that will bring "relief / to my fever burning body." But, the poem concludes, "I drop my hands, / I cannot reach the distant peaks." No longer serving their conventional poetic purpose for Colorado lungers as the source of beauty and inspiration, for Druskin the mountains stand for the goal within sight but beyond his grasp. His freedom is illusory, taunting: the Promised Land lies before him as it had for the Jews in their desert wandering, but he is still chained to the servitude of his disease. As we shall see, the mountains—otherwise providing a vista of hope—loom large in the writing of Yehoash as reminiscent of the heights from which Moses was allowed to see the Promised Land he was forbidden to enter. There Moses died, and, as Samuel A. Silver asks in his English poem "A Wander's Grave," "Who sees the secret place of Moses's tomb?" (*F* 4.3 [1932]).

The locus of servitude and freedom, mortal illness and the possibility of rebirth, a breach in the ordinary course of a human life, a place in the world (and its own world) but not of it, a way-station en route to an uncertain destination—for the Jews, an antiphony of *Ma Tovu* and the mourners' *Kaddish*—the sanatorium is the lungers' purgatory, a "vacant space" preserving no "trace" of those who have passed through. As a patient entering the JCRS, the poet Leivick imagines himself standing *afn shvel* ("on the doorstep," "on the threshold"), calling out, "Open up, gate" (Harshav and Harshav 1986, 737). His stance bespeaks (literally) in Yiddish what we would render in critical parlance as the liminality of the sanatorium experience. Thus, Yehoash's poem "The White Plague" ends with the image of the white plague as the grim reaper, silently harvesting his crop of the "living dead" (*The Sanatorium* [*S*] 1.1 [1907], 30). Thus, too, the opening lines of the English poem "The Lives of the Haunted," contributed to *Hatikvah* (5.1 [1927], 17) by "M.H.M.":

An artificial Quiet
Enforced by signs of "Silence!"

Arrayed in white ——
Cadaverous looking doctors
Shamble to and fro

And thus, too, the punch line of the joke cited above: "Lived here all your life?" "Don't know, haven't died yet." The sanatorium is a borderline, spectral world populated by the "living dead," zombie doctors, the "alive but not living," and the not dead "yet." Derrida famously struggles with the (im)possibility of a living person uttering the sentence: "I am dead." If that living, not-dead-yet person is a JCRS lunger, one of Yehoash's "living dead"—a phrase resonant for Yiddish speakers as the familiar description of one's miserable condition as *toyt-lebendikh*—the sentence is perfectly, if paradoxically, sayable. In the literary tradition of which few JCRS patients will have been aware, the "living dead" speak to us from the epic underworld of Homer or Virgil. For them, the sanatorium figures as its lived equivalent.

Within this liminal space, time is experienced as a medium at once minutely regimented and seemingly endless, an undifferentiated, routinized expanse in which the "normal" progression of events is warped out of shape. In its same-old daily routine—the tubercular version of the film *Groundhog Day*—the sanatorium "clicked off its hours and days like a punch card machine" (MacDonald 1948, 123). In *The Last Lambs on the Mountain* (2010), a semi-autobiographical novel of sanatorium life, Francis Mulhern has her heroine observe that, for her, the "smallest unit of time at the sanatorium was a month. In a world revolving around a disease which ran a long slow course, time was pulled out of shape, elongated and days and weeks were seldom used as measures" (107). The disease took its time to kill you ("inch by inch," says Yehoash in "The White Plague") and even longer to eradicate. In the sanatorium, the ordinary time of one's life was interrupted by a gap that might well last for years. One sanatorium newsletter reprints an article from *The Reader's Digest* written by a physician who points out the benefits of prolonged invalidism: "After a few weeks in bed, time becomes an unimagined luxury.

Time to think, time to enjoy, time to create, time at last to express the best and deepest part of human nature." Illness "pares and rips off the outer parts of life and leaves one with the essence or the very core of it" (*PEP*, December [1938], 13). In the same issue of the *Fluoroscope* as "The Wall," poet-patient J. W. Taff takes a grimmer view of time's (non)passage, in an English poem called "The Day":

The Day
I have gripped each day
And firmly felt its texture
And let it fall
[. . .]
For each was a duplicate
A replica in monotony and routine
Separate links in a single chain
Of pain.

If in its fragrant ambience and its isolation from a contaminated world the sanatorium conjured up the image of a therapeutic utopia, the patients' days spent there, each a "replica" of the last, made it seem to them a *uchronia*: "From *time* and place / No, nothing at all / Is there / But vacant space." The timeless time of the sanatorium will prompt Leivick to conjure up the spirits of Spinoza, Heine, and the deceased poet Dovid Edelshtat—all linked across the years by a single chain of pain.

For a study of sanatorium writing, it is significant that the setting of Taff's poem "The Wall"—"literally" the scene, and the surface, of writing—is the blank wall of the patient's room. In the room where many "have gone before" one might expect to see the writing on the wall—their writing perhaps, as prisoners might write on the wall of their cell, and in that perhaps also some inscription reminiscent of the prophetic "mene, mene, tekel, upharsin" by which the biblical king Balshazzar could (not) read his own fate (Daniel 5: 1–28). But the sanatorium staff would have been scrupulous in cleansing, disinfecting, and otherwise removing any "trace" of the deceased, so that "no single sign" of his life or death remained to disturb the next occupant. The wall bears "no sign" of the poet's dead predecessor, just a "vacant space" to indicate that his death has opened a vacancy for the next lunger, but the "nothing" written there powerfully signifies the dead man's erasure. The "silent face" of the wall faces the poet as the emblem of the silenced dead from whom he is walled off. That there is no "solitary" trace only intensifies the poet's solitude, his isolation from what might otherwise have been—and what may be yet—his companionship with the "many who have gone before." A poem beginning with "nothing" and ending with a "vacant space" might well bracket a profound nihilism: nothing will come of nothing. But the poet is not silenced. Between these two absences *something* is created out of nothing—namely, a poem written on "The Wall" to fill in the blank. Whether in prisons, schools, or monasteries (where the rule of "Silence!" also prevails), walls have always figured as surfaces inviting inscription. Taff's wall may stand as a symbol of the desire motivating all lunger writers, talented or not, to fill the void in their lives and the vacant spaces of their sanatorium newsletters. As we will see, in Leivick's "Ballad of Denver Sanatorium," the dying young patient Nathan Newman dreams that the hand of the Yiddish poet somehow appears to him and "inscribes a poem" on the wall of his room (1940, 506).[11]

The Tuberculosis Patient's Creed

The sanatorium's resemblance at once to a school, a monastery, and a prison is founded on the hard rock of institutional discipline. "The treatment of tuberculosis is essentially a treatment regimen, and

11. Taff was a patient at the National Jewish Hospital in the early forties, a decade after Newman's death in the same institution. Leivick's visits to Newman were part of NJH lore. There is no way of knowing whether Taff had read Leivick's "Ballad," already in print when Taff contributed his own poetry to the NJH *Fluoroscope*, but his "Nothing, nothing, / At all is written / On my wall" reads as a sardonic response to this key passage in the work of the more famous poet.

regimen means *discipline!*"—this from an article entitled "Discipline Life" in *PEP* (November [1937], 21), the Firland Sanatorium magazine whose title stands for "Patient Endurance Principles." Dr. Arthur Rest, as we have seen, places equal emphasis on the patient's "physical" and "morale" resisting power. He goes on to insist that the latter "entails the will to get well, freedom from worry and discouragement, and satisfactory co-operation and obedience" (*EB* 1.3 [1940], 6). To fortify the "morale resisting power," the doctor thus prescribes a concoction of internal and external constraints. To strengthen her body's "resistance" to the disease, the patient must resist the temptation of extreme emotions at either end of the scale, whether "pathogenic" pessimism and despair, or undue excitement (which was thought to "heat the blood"). Self-control in turn is promoted and reinforced by those in control of the institution and its rules, for as an editorial in the *Ear-Bender* makes clear, the sanatorium is "a community in itself" and "[l]ike all communities it must have laws" (1.12 [1941], 1). The "laws," written and oral, typically dictated when (and whether) patients should have bed rest, heliotherapy, activities, visitors, meals, day passes, permission to listen to the radio, mail and telephone privileges, and much else. "Cousinage" (of which more below) was strictly forbidden and could lead to the summary expulsion of patients found *in flagrante* in some secluded nook on the grounds.[12] The "Tuberculosis Patient's Creed" sees it as one's "duty to the sanatorium to obey its rules and regulations": "I ought to have faith, that the staff knows what is best" (*PEP*, October [1938], 9). Similarly, the lunger's "Ten Commandments" include: (2) "Thou shalt bow down thy head in submission to those who serve thee"; (3) "Thou shalt not take the name of thy doctor in vain"; and (5) "Obey thy doctor and nurse" (*PEP*, January [1937], 21). These parodies betray a certain irreverence

12. Of the institutions I discuss, Cragmor was to a certain extent the exception to this draconian rule of law. Like the sanatorium in *The Magic Mountain*, Cragmor attracted a wealthy clientele by offering the ambience and the privileges of a spa.

toward creeds and commandments while implying even more strongly that both the "laws" of the institution and the injunction to take them on "faith" descend from a higher authority.

The disciplinary regime of the tuberculosis sanatorium might thus serve all too easily as a concrete example of the Foucauldian "clinic": a benevolent therapeutic "community" dependent for its functioning on surveillance, unquestioned scientific authority, and the control of an inmate population conditioned to obey—in short, an instance of biopolitics at its most malign. From such a viewpoint, "freedom" comes to mean the patient's ability to police himself (in order to be "free" of pathogenic emotions). The patient must work actively at being passive. "Resistance" (to the disease) comes to mean obedience to authority. In other terms, a system that so deftly turns these words into their Orwellian opposites might be described as a medical dystopia, or again, as a secular theocracy relying for its success on the two-handed engine of shame and guilt to keep the machinery of repression running smoothly. Florence Mulhern's fictional "Ellie" channels her creator's feelings, and doubtless those of many others curing in America's sanatoriums: Ellie hates "all this regimentation. Being told how to spend every minute of every day" (2010, 87–88). I put the case for the prosecution in such sharp relief to emphasize its limitation, as a theoretical sketch rather than a detailed portrait of sanatorium life in all its lived complexity. Those who survived to resume their lives were grateful for the care they had been given, as they were to their doctors (some of whom were themselves recovered lungers) for enforcing the only regime that appeared to offer the best chance for a cure before the development of antibiotics. Some treatments today regarded as bizarre—artificially collapsing a diseased lung to let it "rest," for example, or shining a powerful "Alpine light" down the patient's throat because bacteria prefer to grow in the dark—were undertaken experimentally in the hope of discovering something, anything that would make a difference. In the workshops of the JCRS many patients learned a skilled trade such as printing or bookbinding, or perfected their English. The rules could always be bent if not broken by minor acts of insubordination (reading after lights out, spiriting food or liquor into one's room). Faced with the rule of "Silence!" discontented patients could make their voices heard in the pages of their institutional magazines—a means of effective "resistance" not acknowledged by Dr. Rest.

The Curriculum

If not exactly a college of liberal arts, the sanatorium presented itself as an educational as well as a therapeutic institution, taking care to emphasize how the two went hand in hand. Patients were encouraged to participate in arts and crafts, to hone skills that would better their lives after their release, and, as we have seen, to improve their minds and fortify their spirits by reading, and to aspire to become writers themselves. Yehoash's dictionary project and his sponsorship of literary activities during his years in the JCRS evince his commitment to the institution's cultural life. Patients also needed to be "educated" about their disease so as to be able play their part in fighting it. Like everything else in the patient's daily life, learning required discipline. Betty MacDonald reports that one patient who bridled at the rules "regarded the Pines as a reform school and the nurses as wardens" (1948, 95). As a *PEP* contributor urges, however, "it would be a serious misunderstanding of these strictures to interpret them in a definition of the Sanatorium as a Reformatory": "It cannot be too strongly emphasized that the fight against tuberculosis is in itself an education broader than much that passes under that name. Men and women who survive it are bettered in intellect and character. . . . The sanatorium best provides the curriculum on which must be based behavior in the long and tedious conflict" (February [1937]). One entrant in the NJH literary contest for 1930, Una Ries, submitted an essay on "The Ex-Patient's Role." She explains that "this hospital is an educational institution and instructs hundreds of patients . . . each year in the right way to take the cure and the vital importance of protecting others. The 'graduates' of our Hospital . . . have a wonderful opportunity to convert their associates to a more modern conception of tuberculosis as a curable disease" (*F* 1.9 [1930], 8). In 1926, *Hatikvah* treated its readers to a futuristic "Phantasy à la H.G.

Wells." From a helicopter (the 4426 CE model, presumably) we survey what "used to be a sanatorium twenty-five hundred years ago." A cure for tuberculosis having been found long ago, a part of the old sanatorium is preserved as a memorial. The rest—as if in fulfillment of its educational destiny—has been "transformed into a school of social science" ("And It Will Come to Pass," 4.2, 5). This pedagogical ethos, founded on the assumption that knowledge is itself therapeutic, is arguably the forerunner of our current belief in "education" as the front line of defense against diseases, such as AIDS, for which we have no cure. Recruiting the patient as a collaborator in the process—holding out the hope that the cure will bring with it not only a clean bill of health but a diploma in tubercular studies—appears to blur the hard lines of institutional discipline and to create the impression, if not the reality, that the sanatorium "community" is engaged in a system of progressive education. However, in a 1919 address, S. Adolphus Knopf, "the most widely known and vocal public authority on tuberculosis" (Caldwell 1988, 75), makes the educational pecking order very clear: "The sanatorium," he explains, should be regarded as "a school, a college, where the patients can and must learn many things. . . . The physician is the teacher, the nurse is the assistant teacher, and the patients are the pupils" (Knopf 1919, 9).

Like any "teacher," the physician may at times feel his efforts frustrated by "pupils" who won't follow the lesson plan and who are thus liable to aggravate their condition. Dr. James J. Waring (Gerald Webb's partner in Colorado's Webb-Waring Institute for tuberculosis research) finds that there "are many who will not learn, many who are restless under restraint, who are willful and heedless—spoiled children ever. For these there is no hope." Some few cheaters may survive to boast that they disregarded what Waring calls "the rules of the game," but the rest will surely die. This stern admonition appeared in *PEP* ("Relapse of Recurrence of Activity," December [1936]) as well as in other sanatorium newsletters. Naughty pupils were given to understand that if their conduct did not improve they could be expelled and their places taken by needier and more compliant applicants from the waiting list. After their "gestation period" new sanatorium patients entered a world of nursing care, prescribed bedtimes, obedience, lots of milk, and occupational therapy (at the "Pines," making crocheted doilies and pot holders). In short, they had to adjust to an infantilizing disciplinary system designed to (re) produce and (re)educate the "children" in its care. As a result, child-like sentiment often seeps into patient writing, as in Edward Custer's "Wiegenlied" ("Lullaby"), submitted for the January 1930 literary contest at the National Jewish Hospital (*F* 1.9, 8):

I awoke from sleep
And heard God weeping.
Sleep, child . . .
It is only the wind.

Florence Mulhern's "Ellie" befriends a fellow patient named Fernando who dies just as he seems well enough to leave the sanatorium. Fernando was fond of his guitar, "his puzzles, and his book of magic," Ellie recalls: "Illness had kept him a child with all a child's love of games and tricks, all a child's sweetness." Faced with being thrust out into the adult world, the man-child Fernando cannot survive the transition (2010, 273). In Leivick's "Ballad," as we shall see, "Nathan Newman," the patient (at the NJH) eulogized by the poet, seems more like a helpless and hapless child, here tended by his nurse, than a man in his thirties:

She bathes him as a midwife bathes a child,
A newborn just emerged from mother's womb;
She puts him in a shirt fastened with bows,
And smoothes the bed white, freshening his room. (1940, 510)

The room of this dying new-man, furnished with the few simple things that symbolize his constricted world, seems shrunk to the size of a doll house: " . . . a little closet with a lock, / A small table, and on it, two little books, a thermometer, a pitcher, and a glass" (502).

The starkest example of a sanatorium curriculum concerns a patient population regarded as childlike in the first place. When Colorado Springs' posh Cragmor Sanatorium fell on hard times in the early fifties (antibiotics having by then thinned the ranks of paying customers), the institution entered into a government contract to provide treatment for tubercular Navaho women from reservations in the southwest.[13] Mythologizers of the American frontier had long parlayed the image of Native Americans as physically robust and free of disease—their presumed good health due as much to the land as to their uncorrupted way of life. Reporting on Cragmor's revised mission, the *Colorado Springs Gazette Telegraph* informed its readers in 1958 that "The Navaho Indians live in a mystical, mythical country." But given that "many have never sat in a chair or eaten from a table," *mystical* now appears to mean primitive and unhygienic. As a result, the article goes on to note, tuberculosis now strikes one third of all Navaho families. To address this medical emergency, "the [Cragmor] staff had a theory in 1953 that teaching the Indians to apply sanitation and diet habits used at the sanatorium to their everyday living habits, would make them dissatisfied with poor living conditions on the reservation." The sanatorium thus instituted classes not only in reading and writing, but in housekeeping and in modern cooking methods. To aid in their menu planning, the Navaho women were taken on "buying trips to modern supermarkets." Ellie May John tells the *Telegraph*, "I learn to be clean in the kitchen and how to set a table" (*Telegraph*, March 2, 1958, 1).

Mrs. Dawson, the Cragmor cooking teacher, had explained to another reporter the year before that "in trying to integrate the Indian's way of life into ours, we serve them white man's food here"; this, she concedes, requires "a big adjustment" (*Colorado Springs Free Press*, May 7, 1957, 10). In the wake of Brown v. Board of Education and the Montgomery bus boycott, and with the crisis in Little Rock already brewing, the project of "integrating" the Indian in 1957 takes on a wider cultural resonance, echoing back fifty years to

13. This chapter in Cragmor history is fully recounted in McKay, chapter 6, "The Navajo Indian Decade" (1983, 135–52). I am indebted to his narrative, as well as to records in the Cragmor archive.

the question of Americanizing European immigrants. With tuberculosis nearly eradicated in white America by the late fifties, its presence among the Indians came to mark the difference between the Navajo child-women (who didn't even know how to set a proper table) and their adult instructors in the finer points of etiquette. It also marked the difference between an uncivilized minority and the civilized American majority into which they might be absorbed if they could be cured of their disgusting manners along with, or rather as a means of, being cured of tuberculosis. For several years Cragmor's Navaho patients had their own newsletter entitled *Corn of the Rainbow*—"their own" in the sense that the women's contributions were for the most part translated by white "interpreters" on staff. Even in translation, some modes of traditional therapy were seen to persist as impediments to modern cures. Of the "Navaho Medicine Man," patient Margaret Patero writes in 1954 that "he has saved many lives and still continues to do so for only those that believe in his medicine" (*Corn of the Rainbow* [*CR*], September [1954], 2). To counter such ignorance, an issue of 1956 announced plans by the University of Chicago to sponsor a six-week seminar at Colorado College designed "to give the Indian a general knowledge of their [sic] own background and history, their place in the culture of this country" (*CR*, July [1956], 1). It might be noted that for their occupational therapy, the Navaho women were set the task of making pieces of "traditional" Indian craft, which were then sold to tourists as a means of subsidizing the institution.

Sex

Children, of course, are to be discouraged from having sex, either with each other or with their adult caretakers. This unspoken taboo lurks behind the most draconian rule at virtually every sanatorium. An undated memo to all patients "From the Medical Director" of the JCRS calls attention to the sanatorium's "Rules of Conduct," noting that there is evidence of "a great deal of promiscuous 'necking' going on" and warning that anyone caught in violation will be immediately discharged (JCRS archive). The rule against dalliance of all sorts was understood to be based as much on science as on moralism or on the need to maintain discipline. Tuberculosis could fuel the fires of eros. Passion—indeed, even the thought of passion—was sure to "heat the blood" to a dangerous level for the lunger already suffering, as was typical, from a chronic low-grade fever. Betty MacDonald's fearsome "Charge Nurse" puts the matter succinctly: "In tuberculosis, sex is the worst complication" (1948, 12). Cautionary tales in sanatorium newsletters underscore the danger of romantic entanglements. "Pete" pines away and dies because his girlfriend won't visit (*F* 7.3 [1935]). In the fictional "Case No. 256" by NJS contributor Arno Eldi, a heedless girl sneaks away for "clandestine meetings" with her "blond Romeo." Infatuated, she loses her focus on the cure and—inevitably—dies (*F* 8.6 [1937]). In "Hello, Long Distance," a poem by Betty Richardson, a girl hangs around the telephone in the hallway waiting for a call from "a lad in Brooklyn" who says he "loves me yet." The phone rings, but, as we feared, it's for somebody else (*F* 13.1 [1942]). The lovelorn at Cragmor might find poetical solace in Sue Wallace's "Consolation" (*PEP* 45.1 [1931], 3): "There little girl, don't spoil your eyes, / Don't you know there's not a man alive / Who's worth a woman's tears?"

With dalliance thus strictly forbidden, patients were naturally inclined to dally—to what extent remains unclear, given that sanatoriums did not keep tabs for the record. Clearly, sex always provided a juicy topic for gossip, at least if L. T. B.'s poem in a 1930 Cragmor newsletter can be taken literally:

> Something to do with sex, no doubt.
> Something to do with sex!
> You need have no doubt what the talk's about
> Where gather's the clan all over the San
> By the garbage can, on the upper decks
> It's something to do with sex, old man
> Something to do with sex! (*NES* 38.3 [1930]).

"True Love," an essay by an "Ex-Patient" at NJH, strikes the same note of cheery prurience as the writer expands on the point that "there is none like the sanatorium girl for true romance." Having tried girls on the outside and found them cold and unforthcoming, he finds his thoughts "have unwillingly reverted to colorful Colorado, to the bonnie lassies idolized by the N.J.H. Flouroscope [sic] and a touch of the divine affliction of T.B.":

> I recalled moonlit nights under the shadows of the Rockies and blond and dark-haired girls breathing love, charging the atmosphere itself with deep emotion.
>
> Everything on those nights bespoke true love. On those nights the tired look in her wistful eyes was expressive of a noble soul, a soul that felt keenly the *weltschmertz* of girlhood, the virginal agony for the diminished chances of getting a husband. (*F* 3.7 [1931], 7)

Between these moonstruck lines one can sense something of the urgency and pathos of "true love" in the sanatorium.

Assignations between lungers were fleeting and of necessity furtive. Almost universally in American sanatoriums, people spoke of their lovers as their "cousins," a transparent ruse that fooled no one, least of all the institutional sex police. In Jewish families of the day marriage between first cousins was not unusual. The term nonetheless carried a vague if titillating whiff of incest. With the future uncertain—including the uncertainty of surviving and finding a husband (or wife, or lover) beyond the walls—one lived, and loved, for the day. Marriages were imperiled by separation.[14] Even after a patient's release, in the wider world people tended to avoid close contact, let alone intimacy, with those known to be tainted with TB, asking them for example to eat off paper plates when invited to the home of a friend. When everyone harbored the bacillus, "breathing love" carried no threat to either lover, even to those who could hardly breathe.

14. Jack Gilman, then a patient at the JCRS, filed for divorce from his first wife on the grounds of abandonment when she refused to make the trek from New York to Colorado to be with him. She and their ten-year-old son, Samuel Gilman, then returned to her family in Poland, in the summer of 1939.

Coupling under the shadows of the Rockies was all the more fraught when, as might be the case, a third person was involved: the "lad from Brooklyn" who doesn't call, a husband or wife back home who may or may not remain faithful. Leivick's "Ballad" offers the hint of a triangular—more accurately, a quadrilateral—romance in the suppressed erotic bond between Nathan Newman and his mother-nurse, the love between Newman and the absent sister to whom he writes, and in the poem's brief glance at an "another" who is "something more" than the beloved sister:

> Yes, there is another. But not a sister.
> That is —— a sister and something more;
> He presses her last letter to his lips:
> She loves him, and he loves her even more.
>
> He writes: "It's been so long a wait for you to come,
> And tomorrow you'll be getting on the train,
> So I have taken up my pen in haste,
> To let you know: Don't come to see me here again.
>
> "Don't ever come to see me any more,
> Not even just to bid me once adieu.
> Tear my name out of your mouth, for I've
> Already said to death: yes, take me too." (1940, 503)

The nurse who loves him as a mother, the sister he loves, the one who is not a sister but whom he loves even more (than she loves him)—and finally death, whose proposals he cannot refuse: "Yes, take me too." Love among the lungers, as we will see in chapter 4, will provide the narrative frame of Sholem Shtern's sanatorium novel in Yiddish verse, *The White House*.

Mulhern's *The Last Lambs on the Mountain*, based on her experience as a patient at Saranac Lake in the early 1950s, offers a thinly fictionalized account of such superheated relationships. One woman informs her husband she wants a divorce when she is swept off her feet by the local Lothario. When the Lothario abandons her for another conquest, she commits suicide. "Ellie," Mulhern's protagonist, is a child-woman babied at a distance by her older married lover (he calls her "Kitten"). Just at the point when the lover may or may not leave his wife for his tubercular mistress, he is conveniently killed off in a plane crash, leaving Ellie free to find herself—and eventually to marry her doctor. This fantasy ending is far less persuasive than Ellie's earlier reflection on love at Saranac Lake (2010, 109):

> Dead and dying love affairs were commonplace at the sanatorium. Examples fell with dismal regularity out of its narrow skies, the grief betrayed by silence, the numbing pain laid bare by distant eyes. More often than not the links which let events to their sorry conclusions were similar. Letters and visits that tapered off, bonds that weakened and finally broke under the corrosive action of absence. Just as often the endings were alike, shaped not in hurtful explicit words but by the lethal wound of silence.

The Monastic Life

Inscribed in the rules of the sanatorium, the abstinence from sex as well as the observance of "Silence!" are also imposed on the devout as a keystone of the *regulae* governing a number of monastic orders—unsurprisingly, insofar as sanatoriums, leprosaria, and hospitals themselves can trace their establishment back to the ministrations of the religious. In modern times, Hygeia, the classical goddess of health and hygiene, lent her name as the title of a popular health magazine published by the American Medical Association from 1928 to 1949. The goddess was reincarnated in the 1930s as the poster girl in the war against consumption, appearing on Christmas seals and symbolically spearheading the fundraising campaigns of the anti-tuberculosis movement. The Trudeau archives at Saranac Lake include a photograph of her in the flesh in a meeting with F.D.R. (reproduced in Caldwell 1988, after p. 44). In the photograph very little of her flesh is to be seen, however, for she has evidently traded in her scant Roman drapery for a central-casting nun's habit. She is clothed head to toe in white, her face is shrouded in a modest wimple, and the distinctive two-armed red cross of the movement is emblazoned on her front. In the cover illustration to a 1915 pamphlet entitled "A War On Consumption" (in Caldwell, after p. 44), our newly Christianized Hygeia leads a long procession of the afflicted—to the "war," but evidently also on a pilgrimage to her shrine. She holds aloft a banner with an image of her temple (in fact, the headquarters of the Metropolitan Life Insurance Company that published the pamphlet) in a gesture that recalls the display of images of the Virgin or St. Sebastian at the head of church processions in plague times. Caldwell observes that for Edward Livingston Trudeau, "the cure was not a hospital stay but a way of life . . . a conversion to a nearly religious regimen of health" (48). Searching for just the right spot on which to found his new institution, the founder of the sanatorium movement in America meditated, as Trudeau says in his *Autobiography*, on "the imposing mountain panorama of Saranac" and "yearned for a closer contact with the Great Spirit who planned it all, and for light on the hidden meaning of our troublous existence" (Trudeau 1916, 165–66). Trudeau's yearning prompts him to become an allegorist of the Book of Nature, desiring to uncover the "hidden meaning" of the landscape on which he will found his sanatorium. As a community of lungers seeking the light, patients will presumably benefit not only from the clean Adirondack air but also from an infusion of the Spirit. As disciples of the cure they will (to tip the words of Una Ries into this religious context) "have a wonderful opportunity to convert their associates to a more modern conception of tuberculosis."

Non-Jewish sanatoriums in particular tended to stress the contemplative benefits of an enforced "monastic" retreat. In this spirit a contributor to the newsletter of the (predominantly Christian) Cragmor Sanatorium in Colorado Springs writes that "Segregation, silence, and long periods of time for meditation throw isolated individuals into a medium as nearly perfect for creative thought as one would find in the summer garden of a mountain abbey" (*NES* 51.2). Also in Colorado Springs, the Glockner Sanatorium (under the aegis of the Catholic Sisters of Charity) featured a Gothic chapel with imported stained glass windows and housed the Seton School of Nursing, "founded on the motivating principle of religion in the art of nursing" (Glockner Archives, *Glockner Golden Jubilee*, 1939). The Reverend John S. Żybura, a prominent neoscholastic theologian, "did most of his literary work in philosophy" at Glockner before his death in 1934, having earlier written to a clerical colleague that "there is nothing like suffering to teach one the sacrificial attitude of mind" presumably necessary for his arduous theological labors (Zdrodowski 1949, 81). The patients at Denver's National Jewish Hospital were given a similar piece of free advice by Father Hugh L. McManamin: "Of course," he writes in the *Fluoroscope*, "there are those, not many, who at times rebel against the demands of the cure"; they need to understand that getting well "demands many a sacrifice" (3.8 [1931], 3). Much in the way Trudeau's Christian God morphs into the "Great Spirit" revealed through the Saranac landscape, an anonymous poem in the Glockner Archives sacramentalizes Colorado Springs by evoking in the same breath the town's Edenic Native American past and the baptismal power of her waters:

> The Manitou here dwelt in days gone by
> In crystal springs to cleanse all mortal stains;
> Lone hunters saw their virgin purity . . .
> And hearts are swayed by olive-sceptered Peace.

Pace Hygeia, not everyone bridling under the discipline of the tubercular monastorium was a fan of virgin purity. A Firland nurse barred by the rules from smoking, forbidden to speak to the doctors unless spoken to, and required to abide by a 10:30pm curfew, confided to Betty MacDonald that "if it weren't for Larry [a staff physician to whom she was engaged] I wouldn't stay ten minutes in this nunnery" (1948, 125).

The House of Bondage

Needless to say, the Jewish lungers in the JCRS did not speak the language of "mortal stains" and "virgin purity." Rather, for them, something of the comforting ritual of orthodox observance was built into the regimen of the sanatorium with its insistence on devotion to the cure, and on an elaborate and predictable set of daily rituals over which the physician exercised a quasi-rabbinical authority. Still, unlike Wordsworth's nuns they fretted plenty at what—for them, as for many patients in non-Jewish sanatoriums as well—was not their convent's narrow room but a prison to which they were doomed by an intractable germ. They were not free, however "freely" they could breathe in the pure Colorado air. "From the House of Bondage," a Passover editorial in *Hatikvah*, calls the holiday a time to hope that we "can throw off the shackles of misery which are afflicted by the white plague upon mankind" (4.3 [1926], 9). In "The Psychology of the TB Patient" a physician argues that if "an individual convicted of a crime was given the choice of a few years imprisonment or a death sentence [i.e., by not entering a sanatorium] there is no doubt as to what the preference would be" (*NES* 5.1 [1931], 8–9). Some were not given a preference. Institutions like the Riverside Hospital on New York's North Brother Island—opened in 1850 to treat smallpox, expanded to include a Sanatorium for Pulmonary Diseases in 1903, and later famously the site of Typhoid Mary's confinement—undertook the mission of holding "willfully careless consumptives under forcible detention" (Winslow 1920, 190). But of what "crime" had the Denver lungers been guilty? NJH patient Estelle Taylor asks, "Why are we imprisoned with the four walls of sickness, poverty, disillusionment, hopelessness?" (*F* 4.2 [1932], 5). The same physician who had called prolonged invalidism "an unimagined luxury" argues that "in illness you discover that your imagination is more active than it ever has been" because you are "unshackled by the petty details of existence." Jewish lungers less enamored of this "unshackled" captivity tended to exercise their imagination on the petty details of their existence as prisoners. Abraham Druskin's "Chained," noted above, begins: "Sickness holds me down / Tho free, I lie in bed a captive." M. H. M.'s "The Lives of the Haunted" ends with the image of "grappling souls / Pining / In solitary confinement."

The one "prison" poem I have found in the literature of the non-Jewish sanatoriums would never have been written (I suggest) by a Jewish lunger. Dorothy Dixon's "Grit," published in the Cragmor magazine (*NES* 21.1), offers a recipe for endurance: you can learn to "grin and bear it all,"

> If you can take your temp and find it's risen
> And still refrain from doubting and despair
> If you can learn to like your cell in prison,
> And to forgive the judge who sent you there.

Here, in contrast, is a sampling of texts on the theme of "despair" and "doubt" from the NJH *Fluoroscope* and the JCRS *Sanatorium*. Arnold Lamden crammed his doubts "within the sphere of thought / And sent it rolling to the gates of God; / No answer. . . ." ("Vain Sorrow," *F* 3.11, May [1932]). In a Yiddish poem entitled "A Hoarse Voice from Denver: An Ordinary Jew Poses Questions to the Heavens," G. Zelikevitz—"I, a sick man"—similarly receives no answer to the question of his grief (*S* 2 [1908]). Finally, the concluding stanza of Samuel Silver's "Despair" (*F* 3.12, April [1932]):

> I pray, but a mountain of guilt raised up
> Shutting out from the world unfaltering faith
> And like Cain I am forced in my utter despair,
> To exclaim, "It is more than my spirit can bear."

For Dixon, the injunction to refrain from despair calls upon the virtue of patience, and the need to "forgive" echoes the merciful spirit of the Lord's Prayer—although, oddly in this case, the "judge" to be forgiven is evidently the God who has handed down an unfair sentence in the first place. These sentiments are well suited into a quasi-monasterial institutional framework in which a "sacrificial attitude of mind" validates suffering, and patience erects a bulwark against doubt (if your temp has "risen," so has Our Savior). But for JCRS lungers and those Eastern European Jews in other sanatoriums, the word "cell" inevitably calls up other narrow rooms: the cramped steerage compartments of the Atlantic crossing, the holding pens at Ellis Island and other reception centers, and the haunting cultural—and in some cases, very personal—memory of Czarist oppression and imprisonment. H. Leivick is a case in point.

Coda: Samuel Greenberg: The Deserted Soul

By the time he died of tuberculosis in 1917 at the age of twenty-three, Samuel Greenberg had written more than six hundred poems as well as several plays, an opera, a number of other fragments, and the sketch of an autobiography. None of this material was published during his lifetime, nor is it likely that any of it would have been, save for the coincidence that his manuscripts were later shown to Hart Crane, who was taken with the work of the unfortunate young poet and who borrowed from Greenberg in at least one poem of his own. Largely because of the Crane connection, this untutored but precocious and prolific poet—a "Rimbaud in embryo" as Crane is supposed to have declared (Laughlin 1939, 355)—has been proposed in what little scholarship is devoted to him as an unsung hero of American modernism.[15]

Such a claim might warrant a separate chapter on Greenberg as a Jewish lunger poet, but for three considerations apart from the fact that none of his poems reflects any particular "Jewish" concern. First, as we shall see, only three poems deal directly with his experience as a sanatorium patient—and of these, only "Wards Island Symphonique" is of sustained interest. Second, this Austrian immigrant who came to New York at the age of six knows no Yiddish and writes exclusively in English. As Greenberg was forced to drop out of school at fourteen to go to work, his English is faulty at best. In his autobiography he owns up to this deficiency in a sentence

15. Marc Simon's *Samuel Greenberg, Hart Crane and the Lost Manuscripts* (1978) is the fullest study of the better known poet's debt to Greenberg. The edition of Greenberg's *Poems* (1947) edited by Holden and McManis contains the most generous sample of his work. See also articles by Horton (1936), Rosemont (1989), and Murrell (1920). It was William Murrell, a friend of Greenberg, who first brought his work to the attention of Hart Crane. The Greenberg poems and the passage from the autobiography that I cite in the text I have transcribed from the manuscripts in the Fales Collection at New York University (preserving Greenberg's misspellings) with the exception of "Wards Island Symphonique" where I have relied on the text as it appears in Holden and McManis (1947), 37–38.

that proves the point he is trying to make: "My vocabulary has a great memory for foolish bliss, rather poor in careful selection and of grammatic [sic] assistance unguided." Of his practice of reading "merely to gain letters for the sake of rhyme," he explains that "it was a self-gathering of natural prevention in the ways of life's action." Third, and partly for this reason, much of what Greenberg wrote is disjointed, haphazardly worded, deeply passionate but often virtually incoherent. These qualities have been spun by his admirers as the mark of Greenberg's proto-modernist genius, even as it is hard to deny that one must slog through a great deal of very bad verse along the way. Thus in 1939 James Laughlin, the founder of New Directions, wrote that Greenberg "was crazy about words, crazy about their sounds and shapes and the magical life of association." The following year Louis Untermeyer continued in the same vein: "Long before surrealism became a movement, Greenberg was hypnotizing himself with words in orgies of supersensibility," seeming to "dwell in a state between . . . between sheer hallucination and pure vision."[16] Despite such early critical enthusiasm, the most recent study of Greenberg, by Hart Crane's editor Marc Simon, appeared in 1978. The poet discovered with such excitement when his link to Crane came to light has been undiscovered again for more than thirty years in the scholarly world, although in the world of New York poetry he was known to Elizabeth Bishop (who recommended him to Robert Lowell), as well as to John Ashbery and Frank O'Hara, who invokes Greenberg's name in the poem "Cornkind" (1971, 387).

Why, then, Greenberg—the poet for whom sound trumps sense and quantity trumps quality? To his brother Daniel he writes: "This warm, drowsy pain – send me a fountain pen soon" (Holden and McManis 1947, xviii). The answer lies in the intense relation, at once therapeutic and pathological, between Greenberg's "pain" and his

16. Cited in *Samuel Greenberg: American Poet* (http://www.logopoeia.com/greenberg).

"pen." Nearly everything we have of Greenberg's poetry—and we have a great deal of it—was written from his hospital sickbed during the last four years of his short life; earlier, when he submitted a citizenship application at the age of nineteen, he listed his occupation as "Painter of Portraits (Artist)," and he filled sketchbooks with very good pencil drawings of heads, some copied from paintings in the Metropolitan Museum. Beginning with 1913 when his illness "closed in with its careful teeth" Greenberg set off on his last woeful odyssey from hospital to hospital, with brief periods of intermission that only landed him back in the next institution in worse shape: a year in Manhattan State Hospital on Ward's Island, then to Montefiore Hospital in the Bronx, then to St. Anthony's Hospital in Woodhaven (where he underwent an operation to remove a tubercular kidney), and finally, in his last year, to the Sea View Hospital on Staten Island, at that time one of the largest sanatoriums in the country (xvii). By their sheer abundance his manuscripts (housed in the Fales Collection at New York University since 1964) leave the impression that during these years he must have written every day—written compulsively, endlessly, one is tempted to say breathlessly, unencumbered by syntax, punctuation, and spelling, making use of any scrap of paper that came to hand, from composition books, loose sheets of all sizes, note pads, and postcards, to the blank spaces on a medical examination form, and in one instance even a patient intake questionnaire from Bellevue Hospital. Hallucinatory and hypnotic, barely in control of his medium, and driven by a compulsion to write no matter what or when, Greenberg seems less in possession of language than possessed by it.

In "Nurse Brings Me Medicine," one of his three sanatorium poems, Greenberg responds to the proffered potion: "Medicine? / For me! God, twenty years old! / Medicine? I'd leave it to thee! / The truth is a draught." Greenberg's "truth" is in his drafts, the only "draught" from which he draws sustenance. The sheer ability to keep writing, to tap into the energy of words for their own sake, to conjure their "magical life," is proof enough that the patient is truly alive. The loss of one's voice is the harbinger of death. Thus, the second sanatorium poem, "Dying Young Patient," begins: "Speechless? How young thou art! / The voice of death has sought thee." The Palgrave Anthology, one of the few books at Greenberg's bedside, evidently schooled him in the art of the exclamation point, in the use of "thou" and "thee" and "O," and in such poetical contractions as 'pon and 'een. It also prompted him to establish a personal relationship with the late-Romantic muse. But in a turn wholly his own, the poet does not seek out the muse: the muse finds him. Speechlessness is the voice of death or, put otherwise, death—in a dark parody of the breath of inspiration—has its own "voice" that speaks for you when yours falls silent. So, too, in the poem "Expression," it is not the "man" who knows how to express himself:

> Expression! Like a beast thou knowest the man!
> Who trails in ailment 'pon this vast~~ly~~ [sic] globe
> And ruins lives beyond the common stand [.]

"Expression" must be invoked, but once called upon, it is expression that knows the man. It is the "man" who seemingly "trails in ailment" and "ruins lives," and yet Greenberg's shaky syntax leaves open the possibility that Expression "trails" the man as a "beast" trails its prey and so "ruins lives." In the last years of Greenberg's ruined life, these moments in his poetry suggest that expression is less a gift of the gods in response to an inner impulse than a beastly force with some kind of knowledge the writer himself does not possess, and by which he is pursued to his ultimate ruin. The strikethrough in "vastly" suggests a struggle at the micro level between what the man would say and what Expression demands. In this relation to writing, the "self" is always in jeopardy. Greenberg's ceaseless writing seems haunted by the anxiety that if there is no writing, there is no self to have written, or to have written itself. His poem "To Self" contains the line "what shall / Youthfull [sic] charm waste? O self not thine age; thy ghost!" To judge from the extent of the Fales Archive, Greenberg preserved every scrap of his writing, not so much as a legacy perhaps, but rather as the material evidence of his tubercular self-depletion, the simulacrum of the self he poured into it. As the writer himself wastes away, his writing thrives and grows fat. Otherwise, thy "self" is already "thy ghost."

The title of Greenberg's most ambitious and intermittently stunning sanatorium poem, "Wards Island Symphonique," recalls his earlier passion for music.[17] Here, a line like "With a whirl of angle [angel?] puff purple clouds" or a phrase like "winkles its woven solitude" captures the poet's ear for pure sound—"a music sense trembles an emotion." He writes,

> as Birds chirp
> To one another —— in their monotous [sic] note
> A dream of spiritual necessity —— and wild Fancy —— that
> Hums its way —— when at the Islands Bank
> In a trance ——.

At the same time, the poem comes closer than most of Greenberg's other verse to the features of external reality: on holidays, visitors cross to the island by ferry with parcels for the patients who anxiously await their arrival. Once we untangle the syntax we learn that "all visiters [sic] are welcome / Except those of serious condition can Be visited." And then later, to the sound of a loud whistle, the boat departs again for Manhattan. There are the island's "Paved roads," a modern improvement that somehow seems "strange," perhaps because at another moment the Island morphs into "The melted ruins of Egytian [sic] cursed its ghostly colors." We also see the "Nurses in their coloured garments and linear caps." These are moments, as the poet says uncharacteristically, of "Simply relating." What's missing here is any correspondingly firm sense of the poet's presence in this scene. "'Tis silent!" and the spirit has / Fled." Among "the shuffled minds / Strange an emotion – we fear there are none." The "Buildings seem empty," a void echoed in "The deserted soul / Of corrupted Brains and visions Bent." Like the deserted "Ruins of Egytian," both

17. The text of Greenberg's "Symphonique" can also be found online at http://logopoeia.com/greenberg/ghost.html#wards.

the Wards Island Hospital and the consciousness that performs the poem's "shuffled" and "Bent" symphonique are "ghostly." Greenberg's final poem, sent in a postcard to his brother Daniel and dated March 14, 1917, reads in full: "There is a loud noise of Death where I lay; / There is a loud noise of life far away."

The three Yiddish poets to be revisited in the following chapters will have known nothing of Samuel Greenberg. But his example reveals the symptoms of sanatorium writing *in extremis*. Sanatorium writing is ghost writing, haunted by the memory if not by the spirits of the dead who have been removed in the stealth of night, leaving only their empty beds to be occupied by the next patient. Even in the most optimistic paeans to hope or to the beauties of nature, the sanatorium poet writes *for* himself and his reader, but always implicitly *against* the specter of death that will bring the writing, and the writer, to an end. Like the chirping of the birds on Wards Island, sanatorium writing is a "spiritual necessity."

2

Yehoash and the Yiddish *Hiawatha*

Our Byron

Of the four major projects completed or undertaken by Solomon Bloomgarten (1870–1927) while he was chasing the cure in Colorado, the most improbable would seem to be his Yiddish translation of Longfellow's *The Song of Hiawatha* (1910). Over his nine years as a recovering tubercular, Bloomgarten, who wrote under the pen name "Yehoash," also published his first volume of *Collected Poems* (1907), collaborated with Dr. Charles Spivak, the founder and director of the JCRS, on a new Yiddish dictionary that appeared in 1911, and began work on the Yiddish translation of the Hebrew Scriptures that would preoccupy him for the rest of his life. The leisure afforded by life in the JCRS accounts in part for this extraordinary burst of activity. In New York, the writer had been forced to support himself with odd jobs. Just before the onset of his illness he was employed as a "bookkeeper in the glass factory" of a distant cousin where, as his daughter Evlin Yehoash Dworkin writes in her memoir *My Father Yehoash*, the "glass dust ate into his lungs" (1952, 12). These last three projects—the collection of verse, the dictionary, and the Yiddish Bible—comport with Yehoash's single vocation as a poet, philologist, and translator. A short poem appended to an early photograph of the young poet-scholar (figure 3) reads in translation: "Beautiful gleaming colors / Devoid of thought can never / Create a poem."

His Yiddish rendering of the Hebrew Scriptures in particular—a work both scholarly and poetic—Yehoash would regard as an

3. The young Yehoash, "our Byron." One of a series of photos of Jewish writers originally issued as postcards.

endeavor of central cultural importance. But a Yiddish *Hiawatha*? And in 272 pages of trochaic tetrameter, hardly a conventional form for Yiddish poetry no matter how skillfully it reproduces the beat of Longfellow's verse? What "thought" might justify such a task, and how might the *Hiawatha* be understood both in relation to Yehoash's other projects and to the environment of the sanitarium in which it was conceived and completed?

Born in Lithuania and trained in the famous Volozhin Yeshiva at Vilna, Yehoash emigrated to the United States in 1890. In an anecdote reported by his daughter Evlin Dworkin and repeated in nearly every account of Yehoash's career, we are told that "On the way he passed through Warsaw," where he showed some of his early verse to I. L. Peretz. The distinguished Yiddish poet and dramatist "immediately became enthusiastic over the new poet and referred to young Yehoash as 'our Byron'" (Dworkin 1952, 12).[1] In 1899, Yehoash arrived in Denver, as nearly every new TB patient would subsequently, "dispirited, moneyless, with a death sentence hanging over his head." Twenty years he told his daughter that "if he were fated to die soon, he wanted to die surrounded by the Rockies rather than New York's tenement houses." What awaited him in Denver was not only his physical recovery (albeit incomplete, for he remained in fragile health until his death at the age of fifty-seven), but a spiritual rebirth despite his "constant companionship with the Reaper" (Dworkin 1952, 11). Together with Dr. Spivak he was instrumental in establishing the JCRS, which formally opened its doors in 1904. A tireless supporter and publicist for the new institution—Dworkin says the JCRS "was born on a street corner with Yehoash speaking from the top of a soap box"—Yehoash undertook an east-coast fundraising tour in 1908 and, serving on the Board of Directors, was noted for "his life-long devotion to the Sanatorium" (Dworkin 1952, 13; see also Abrams 2009, 100, for the tour).

In addition to working with Spivak on the dictionary, Yehoash helped to launch *The Sanatorium*, the JCRS's first newsletter for patients and staff, which offered not only "reports and statistics related to the JCRS but medical advice, human interest stories, and poetry" contributed by patients (Abrams 2009, 101). Such publications in effect were instrumental in forging the tubercular community into a literary community, one in which poems, sketches, jokes, anecdotes and (crucially) gossip shared the same space with medical advice. As we have seen, standard medical advice saw the forum of the newsletter as itself therapeutic, encouraging creative activity, contributing to the patients' psychological well-being through a sense of solidarity with their fellow "lungers," and thus reinforcing their

1. The details of Yehoash's life and career are culled from a number of sources including Abrams (2009), Madison (1968), Goldstick (1952), Orlinsky (1941), and *Jewish American Literature: A Norton Anthology* (2001). The Yehoash-Spivak dictionary is available in facsimile online: http://archive.org/details/idisherer-bukhenhoospivuoft (accessed April 1, 2013).

commitment to the "cure" in an age when any real cure was beyond the doctors' reach. A staple of sanatorium life everywhere, newsletters were replete with poems and stories, some satiric, most uplifting, and many incompetent. Nonetheless, they offer a rich context for the more accomplished efforts of writers like Yehoash who lived and worked among the patient-versifiers or who, like H. Leivick after him at the JCRS, conducted something like a creative writing workshop.

From a broader perspective, as Sunny Yudkoff has shown, the campaign inaugurated by Yehoash to put the newly formed JCRS on the map of Jewish philanthropy promoted the image of the sanatorium not only as a place of healing but as a wellspring of Yiddish poetry in the Rockies, as if the purity of the air and the grandeur of the mountain peaks might invigorate the writer and inspire his work. The sanatorium's newsletters, available by subscription nationally for a dollar a year, featured poems by a number of patient-versifiers over the years. JCRS patient Lune Mattes, who published four volumes of Yiddish poetry before his death in 1929, struck just this ecstatic note: "I lift up my poem / in song to you Colorado, / my Colorado."[2]

The Dictionary

When the Yehoash-Spivak dictionary came out in 1911 there was little chance it would capture the market for Yiddish reference books as had Alexander Harkavy's monumental *Yiddish–English Dictionary*, first published in 1893 and subsequently revised and reprinted many times over the next forty years in formats large and small (including a *Pocket Dictionary* in 1898). The sixteenth edition of Harkavy (1928) incorporates the original Yiddish preface of 1893 and that of the edition of 1910, which was fresh off the press just months before the Yehoash volume appeared. Why, then, the need for yet another dictionary?

2. This broader perspective was opened for me by Sunny Yudkoff's lecture "American Yiddish Literature: A Tubercular Perspective" delivered at New York's YIVO Institute for Jewish Research, April 16, 2013. The line from Mattes (Yudkoff's translation) is from his poem "Colorado" (1923). I am grateful to her for his insight.

Harkavy's prefaces announce that in its comprehensive scope the dictionary "contains not only words in common use but those that appear in scholarly books." It will thus prove necessary to "everyone of whatever class or line of work, or whatever level of education": to the businessman, the worker, the teacher, the doctor, the judge, the philosopher, even to the "sportsman." A quick glance through the text confirms Harkavy's attention to a "scholarly" vocabulary: randomly, one finds Yiddish definitions for "hydrographer," "hypostatic," "tenebrosity, "preterition," "mitrailleuse," "heteroclitical," "rocambole" ("the Spanish shallot") and even a term presumably of use to doctors, "revomit." From Harkavy, the shoemaker could learn the English word "sole," the itinerant old-clothes dealer the word "peddler," and the metaphysician the word "cosmogony." As an indispensable resource in the process of Americanization, the dictionary promised every Yiddish-speaking immigrant the complete practical and theoretical vocabulary required not only for basic linguistic competence in the new land but for access to the heights of commerce and the learned professions. For "the great Americaniser" (as Harkavy is commemorated in the introduction to a current reprint of the 1928 dictionary), the road between Yiddish and English still ran both ways: greenhorns had to learn English, but they should also "cultivate their own language with pride, seriousness and devotion" (Katz 1988, x–xi). Nonetheless, the assimilationist thrust of Harkavy's dictionary stands in sharp contrast to Yehoash's conviction that the vitality of Yiddish as a medium of cultural solidarity depends not on expanding the word stock to include concepts in other languages but on excavating the common Hebrew roots from which all varieties of Yiddish spring—moving inward to recover an ancient core rather than outward to increase the circumference.[3]

3. To be perfectly precise, the biblical word stock adopted into Yiddish should be called its *loshn kodesh* component—i.e., taken from the "holy language"—rather than its "Hebrew" component, since the latter word conventionally refers to the modern Hebrew language.

There would have been few cosmogonists in Yehoash's orbit, whether in the Volozhin Yeshiva, the glass factory in New York, or the JCRS in Denver. Although his dictionary has no interest in either the Americanization or the professional advancement of the reader, the commitment he shares with Harkavy to Yiddish as a living language is firmly imbedded in the dictionary as in everything he wrote. As a poet before he was a dictionary maker, Yehoash would look askance at the dryer side of lexicography, cautioning the noted philologist and fellow Velozhin alumnus Israel Davidson: "Beware the library dust. . . . The book world and all studies of ologies and osophies have value only in their intrinsic relation with, and through their direct or indirect influence on, the healthy, fresh and pulsating life" (quoted in Madison 1968, 168). The comment reflects a vitalist strain in Yehoash's poetry, which attends to moments when, as he says, "the heart of each mute pebble comes to life" (quoted in Goldstick 1952, 17). Where is the pulsating life of Yiddish to be found if not at its very core in the holy language? Yehoash's poem "Nurture," echoing Numbers 20:9, instructs the reader, "And if you enjoin it so, / Each rock with honeyed sap will flow" (lines 5–6, trans. Goldstick 1952, 55). In light of the special focus of Yehoash's dictionary, it is significant that he should have shared this concern with Davidson, a Hebraist rather than a Yiddishist and the editor of a four-volume *Thesaurus of Mediaeval Hebrew Poetry.* For the Yehoash-Spivak dictionary of 1911 is entitled *Yiddish Dictionary: Containing all the Hebrew (and Chaldaic [i.e., Aramaic]) Words, Expressions, and Proper Names Which Were Used in the Yiddish Language, providing also their Pronunciation, Accent, and with Examples from Words and Proverbs in which they Appear.* There is nothing English about this project: the dictionary defines in Yiddish the meaning of those words in the same language derived from Biblical Hebrew, words whose meaning may not readily apparent to speakers unschooled in the Torah, in the traditional liturgy, or in the Talmud (which is written in Aramaic). Enjoined by Yehoash, the "honeyed sap" of Biblical Hebrew will flow through the dictionary into the stream of contemporary Yiddish.

In publishing what a reviewer in 1912 heralded as "the first complete dictionary of the Hebrew elements in Yiddish" (Ember 1912, 214), Yehoash and Spivak had two principal goals in mind: first, to give "a full and sufficient collection of all the Hebrew words [in Yiddish] in order to provide material for scholars and philologists to pursue their research" into the processes by which Yiddish acquired its Hebrew substrate. The second goal was to meet the "long-felt needs" of a different, and much larger, class of readers: "The compilers have kept in mind the great number of Yiddish readers and writers who have had no instruction in Hebrew in their younger years" (Yehoash, foreword to 1926 ed., ix). The former goal was designed to put a valuable linguistic resource into the hands of a few specialists. The latter reached beyond the advancement of scholarship to engage a complex set of cultural and political issues, including the relationship between Yiddish and Hebrew and the potential of a common language as the bedrock of Jewish identity. These issues raised in turn the most fundamental question for a diverse immigrant community faced on the one side by the lure of assimilation, and on the other by the waning influence of a traditional religious training in Hebrew that might have once been taken for granted (at least for men) in Ashkenazic Europe: What does it mean to be a Jew?

Yehoash estimates that eighty percent of Yiddish (in its many Ashkenazic dialects) comes from the Slavic languages and from German, and the remaining twenty percent (with changes in orthography and pronunciation, but not in meaning) from Hebrew. In addition he notes that some hundreds of thousands of Sephardic Jews speak the Spanish-Yiddish amalgam known as Ladino (foreword to 1926 ed., vii). Nonetheless, Yehoash finds that whenever a Jew meets another Jew, whatever their geographical origins or the regional flavor of their Yiddish, the two of them will share a fund of words (such as *Torah*, *mitzva*, *yom-tov*, *khokhma* [wisdom], *tzedaka* [righteousness], and, unsurprisingly, *meshuga* and *gonif*) appropriated from Hebrew (v). The one common and stable element in all these varieties of Yiddish—the only element, indeed, that underwrites Yiddish *as* a stable language—is its enduring Hebrew component. Only because

Yiddish draws its Hebrew vocabulary from the most ancient and venerated sources—"the Torah, Talmud, midrash, *Tfilot* [the central body of liturgy], *Slichot* [penitential prayers] and *Kinot* [the book of Lamentations]"—can it find expression for the most important concepts language can address: matters of faith, knowledge, truth, ethics, justice, hope and despair. Such was his faith in Hebrew as a language pulsating with life at the heart of Yiddish that Yehoash believed the language would grow to meet contemporary needs not by Yiddishizing ambient English words ("telefon," subway "tokn") but by expanding its Hebrew vocabulary. In 1910 he could not have foreseen that his prediction would come true in quite a different sense with the invention of modern Hebrew, even as six million European Yiddish speakers (out of Yehoash's estimate of ten million) went up in smoke, and as Yiddish retreated into enclaves of the ultraorthodox—and, latterly, into the academy, where today it survives on artificial life support. By isolating the Hebrew words at the foundation of Yiddish, providing a guide to their pronunciation in phonetic Yiddish, and defining them in the common parlance, the dictionary performs a double gesture in the relation of Hebrew and Yiddish. On the one hand, it secularizes the Hebrew, making it available in contemporary Yiddish to speakers severed from religious tradition, and who for that reason no longer have access to the crucial twenty percent of their own language. On the other hand, it re-sacralizes the Yiddish, restoring its "historical meaning and national character," stabilizing it against change by rooting it in a holy language "as old as the Jewish people" itself (viii).

But what is required for Jews to be "the Jewish people"? Yehoash's word for people (*folk*) is singular. What defines the singularity of the Jewish people at a time when the American Jewish "community" is populated by the observant and the militantly secular, by socialists and bundists and anarchists, Zionists and anti-Zionists, and—to the further peril of Yiddish as a binding force—the German Jews for whom Yiddish was nothing more than a corrupt dialect of *Hochdeutsch*? Yehoash was not alone in arguing that Yiddish (his Yiddish, its ancient Hebrew characters restored) could circumscribe the "national" character of a people without a nation. Harkavy, too, saw Yiddish (his Yiddish, expanded to accommodate the language of assimilation) as a medium of cultural solidarity in "an era characterized by bitter infighting, political squabbling, and ideological polarization in the immigrant Jewish community" (Katz 1988, x–xi). But for Yehoash the binding force of Yiddish lay not in the vagaries of regional dialects but in its stable core of Hebrew. Even more, it appears that the dictionary would serve the same purpose even for Jews who spoke no Yiddish: "For Jews all over the world, and from earliest times to today, *whatever their language*, they always made use of a greater or smaller number of Hebrew words in their interactions with one another" (Yehoash, preface to 1911 ed., 1; emphasis mine). Remarkably—and ironically from today's point of view—Yehoash's correspondent Israel Davidson could claim in 1911 that the "importance of Yiddish as a literature is growing from year to year. . . . In the short space of a quarter of a century Yiddish literature has made such rapid strides that it bids fair to outstrip modern Hebrew—not of course in all its branches—but at least in poetry and fiction" (285). Ruth Wisse writes of this period that "the *landsmannschaften*, the Jewish national parties, the social welfare organizations, and the powerful Yiddish press, tried to provide the social and ideological underpinnings for communal cohesion, and looked to such poets as Bovshover, David Edelstadt, Morris Rosenfeld, Abraham Liessin, [and] Yehoash as a persuasive arm of this enterprise" (1976, 266).

The Yiddish Bible

As he was finishing the dictionary, Yehoash had already begun work on his Yiddish translation of the Bible—a long range endeavor directed to the same end as the dictionary, namely to make the sacred text available to readers with little or no Hebrew. If Jews were the people of the Book, and if the language of the people was to be Yiddish, then the Book in Yiddish would doubly fortify the constitution of the *volk*. Pieces of Yehoash's translation would appear in the Yiddish newspaper *Der Tog* (The Day) over the following years, but the complete Pentateuch was published only in 1927, the year of

Yehoash's death. According to Madison, "The impulse came to him as early as 1904, and in 1907 he began to realize it. By 1910 he had completed [his] translation of Isaiah, Job [a text surely meaningful to one enduring his own undeserved misfortune as a victim of TB], Song of Songs, Ruth and Ecclesiastes." But this first draft "seemed to him imperfect and he destroyed it." He would now embark on an arduous course of research "to find in old tomes, folklore, and folk speech the idiomatic Yiddish words that rendered exactly the original Hebrew meaning" (1968, 180). For Yehoash, the Yiddish Bible would stand as a companion to—indeed, as the fulfillment of—the project begun with the dictionary. Like the stable Hebrew core at the center of a constantly changing Yiddish vernacular, the text of the Bible reveals "eternity in the midst of temporality": "Leaves fall, leaves sprout, and the trunk remains and upholds the *aynikayt* of the tree" (Yehoash, preface to 1941 ed., i–iii; my translation). The image is deeply resonant of Yehoash's design. *Aynikayt* means "uniqueness," "integrity," and "identity." The "leaves," in Yiddish *bleter* as in English, suggest at once the passage of time (to everything there is a season), the pages of the book, and the generations of the people of the book, who ripen on the various branches of Biblical Judaism, and then fall. Yehoash's word for "trunk" (*shtam*) also means race or tribe. His compilation of individual words in the dictionary would provide the philological database for translating the entire word of God into Yiddish, imbuing the *mamaloshn* (the "mother-tongue") with the authority and reverence of the *loshn kodesh* (the "holy tongue," the language of the fathers), but with a feminizing touch, making it available to Yiddish speakers who could no longer easily understand the Hebrew but who had learned Yiddish at their mothers' knee.

Yiddish translations of scripture, in part or in whole, date back to the sixteenth century. Early versions include those by Elia Levita (1544), Yekutiel Ben Isaac Blitz (1679), and Joseph Witzenhousen (1687)—not to mention Moses Mendelssohn's 1783 rendition into elegant German (much reviled by orthodox speakers of Yiddish). A Yiddish translation of the Pentateuch dating back to the seventeenth century was included in the *Ze'enah u-Re'enah*, a devotional manual for women, who could not be expected to read Hebrew. Yehoash has this last text in mind when he writes that in addition to striving for accuracy—"A Yiddish TaNaCh should not add to or diminish [the original] insofar as this is possible when one pours water from the vessel of one language into another"—the translation should have the same *haymishkayt* (homeliness, familiarity, comfort) as the language in the *Ze'enah u-Re'enah* (preface to 1941 ed.). Yehoash's translation would supersede them all, both in its exactitude and in its use of the current, idiomatic language. This project he considered his life's work, conceived at the JCRS, published in New York after twenty years of grinding toil, and supplemented by his daughter's publication of a final two volumes and one volume of Yehoash's *Notes on the Bible* in 1941, "completing a cycle," as she writes, "begun fifty years ago in the Rocky Mountains of Colorado" (Dworkin 1952, 15).[4]

On the Mountain

Yehoash told his sister that "to translate one sentence just as I would wish, it gives me more pleasure than the writing of ten poems" (Madison 1968, 180). Imagining that he was rendering the word of God for the masses, he did not foresee the day when copies of his Bible translation would be available mainly in specialized collections of Judaica, while his poetry continues to appear in collections, albeit in translation, most recently in *Jewish American Literature: A*

4. The publication history of the Yehoash Bible is complicated: "In 1922 he agreed to publish, at the rate of several chapters per week, in . . . *Der Tog*, but by the end of 1925 more than half of the Bible . . . had been made available to the public." Yehoash lived "just long enough to see in print the first two volumes, constituting the Pentateuch." The Bible was published in eight volumes by the Jewish Publication Society in 1937, followed in 1938 by a *Folks Oisbabe* (Popular Edition) in two volumes, and a children's Bible based on his translation, the *Chumesh far Kinder,* in 1940. In 1941 under his daughter's supervision there appeared a "bi-glot Bible in two columns, the Masoretic text of the Hebrew and his Yiddish translation facing each other" (Orlinsky 1957, 245–47).

Norton Anthology (2001). But all three of Yehoash's projects are of a piece. If the Bible translation draws upon his philological expertise as a dictionary-maker, it also reflects the deeply literary sensibility of the poet, not only in those sections of scripture formally poetic but throughout in the clarity and flow of the style, capturing what Yehoash calls the "rhythm and music" of the sacred text (Preface to 1941 ed.). In turn the themes and the language of his Bible translation are echoed in his poetry.

Of course most Yiddish verse invokes the language of scripture to a greater or lesser extent. For Yehoash, the story of Abraham is especially resonant. Jewish schoolchildren conventionally began Torah study not with the creation but with Genesis 12:1, where (in my translation of Yehoash's Yiddish) Abraham answers the divine call to "leave his country, his people, and his father's house" and journey to "a land that I will show you." For Abraham to undertake the journey he must first be uprooted from his fatherland and walk by faith alone toward a destination as yet unknown. The strength of his faith is to be tested again in Genesis 22:1–2. Having been severed from a father, he is now commanded (in apparent violation of God's earlier promise to "make of you a great 'folk'") to cut his own son's throat: "Take your son, your only son whom you love, Isaac, and go to the land of Moriah, and bring him there as a burnt offering on one of the mountains I will tell you of." Again, the destination is to be revealed only later. On which mountain will the promise of a "great people" be fulfilled—paradoxically, by a sacrifice that obliges the patriarch to kill off any hope of a future generation? Genesis 12 and Genesis 22, according to the rabbis the two most difficult tests imposed upon Abraham, are linked thematically by the command to "go" and by the compensatory but vague promise of destination "I will show you" or "I will tell you."

The larger story of the Torah moves from exile to the promise, and then through a period of enslavement and wandering until, at the end, the people are ready to enter the promised land—which, however, Moses is only allowed to see from the top of Mount Nebo. These final verses of the Torah in Deuteronomy 34 recapitulate

Genesis 12, but in reverse. Earlier, Abraham was set on a journey toward a land he could not see. Now Moses, at the end of the journey, can see the Promised Land he cannot enter. Two other mountains rise up from the Biblical landscape: Ararat, where the faithful are saved from destruction after the flood, and Sinai where Moses receives the law but then barely saves the people from destruction at the hands of an angry God when, through a lack of faith, they revert to idolatry. While these two peaks represent events that affect the whole people, the temptation of Abraham on Mount Moriah poses an isolated and profoundly disturbing test of one man's obedience. The scene on Moriah powerfully condenses all the themes—dislocation, an apparent death sentence, a test of faith, and a providential redemption—played out at length in the five acts of the Pentateuch, and again in the middle years of Yehoash's life in the Rockies.

Mountains loom large in Yehoash's imagination, as they do in the landscape of the JCRS (figure 4).

His own journey, like that of his fellow patients at the JCRS and of many other tubercular itinerants as well, led him into a double exile: from his father's house in Lithuania to the land of promise in America, and thence, afflicted by disease, to the Colorado mountains and a sanatorium imagined at the Seder table as new Egyptian captivity. There, at least, he could make his destiny his choice, determined to "die surrounded by the Rockies rather than New York's tenement houses." But the prospect can be terrifying. In the Yiddish poem "Amid the Colorado Mountains," written at the JCRS, the poet looks up to the mountains where

> a thunderstorm
> is ready to commence.
> The black clouds, like attacking knights,
> come on in regiments.
>
> It flashes forth! The blades unsheathe,
> a savage sorrow howls
> and more than once reverberates
> from the abyss's bowels . . .

4. Lungers receiving "heliotherapy" at the JCRS, against the background of the Rockies. Before antibiotics, sunlight was no worse than any other treatment available, although skin cancer was a possible side effect. Photograph courtesy of Beck Archives, Special Collections, CJS and University Libraries, University of Denver.

> Already every dale can feel
> a gruesome tumult rise,
> And on my face the first warm drop
> has fallen from the skies . . .
>
> So I am too am [sic] anointed now,
> and feel at home with cloud
> and titan-peak, with lightning-flash
> and thunder roared aloud. (ll. 13–28, in Chametzky et al. 2001, 140–41; trans. Aaron Kramer)

The storm is "savage," abysmal, "gruesome," sublime in its terror. The "attacking knights" seem to recall a dark vision of Cossack predators.

Yet the poet is "anointed" by the "first warm drop." Amid the tumult, indeed empowered by its energy, he feels "at home." A longer poem from the same period looks back from the Rockies toward the gentler pastoral landscape of the Catskills, those "verdant mountains" the poet left behind on his westward trek. Those were mountains "where light and shade are sweet / Where tree and bloom at every turn / With close friendship delight the eye and heart," and "Where dwells the spirit of serene meditation." The Catskills can, in memory, "Banish the phantom of those monster mounds, / Of that cold, towering world of rocks." Yet this pleasant recollection is far overpowered by

> the cold, bald, lofty Rocky Mountains
> With their white snow-turbans upon their peaks
> That there in my far-off western home
> In naked grandeur stare against the sun,
> Where the eagle sits upon his rocky throne
> In cruel, silent loneliness,
> And in his ice-covered tower lives
> The wild prairie hurricane. (ll. 33–34, 11–18, in Cooperman 1967, 10–11; trans. Jehiel B. Cooperman)

In both poems Yehoash is "home," finally, perched like the eagle in "cruel, silent loneliness," and yet like the eagle, "enthroned"—anointed by the rain, a monarch in an "ice-covered tower." But the fantasy of a titanic power displayed in the flash of lightning and the reverberation of thunder—even its reality in the power of poetry—can barely compensate for the weakness of the tubercular flesh. In an extraordinary vision included in the 1907 *Collected Poems*, Yehoash dreams that a mighty angel "flies from one heavenly peak to another," his "broad, white wings outspread." Dramatizing a verse from the burial *Kaddish* ("He will give life to the dead and raise them to eternal life"), Yehoash's angel issues the call with a blast of his "gleaming trumpet":

> Stand up, you dead, from your cold grave
> And rise up from your deathly cavern

> Put on a new body, a new skin,
> Stretch your limbs, powerful and sound.

But like Adelaide Crapsey's grave dwellers, the "dead have forgotten the light" and cannot answer the call:

> They no longer can believe in life and strength,
> Lazy, contented with the peace of the grave
> They will not rise up from their bed of worms. ("A Desolate Dream," 371–72)

The regimen of the sanatorium called for those even at death's door to maintain the cheerful spirit thought essential to their cure. Bed rest was the patient's work; life and strength depended upon his will to survive as much as upon his willingness to endure the routine of the institution. The poet's futile injunction to "Put on a new body" glances at once at the unlikelihood of the resurrection and at the spiritual weakness of those who will not rise up from their beds because they "can no longer believe in life and strength." Yehoash's word "lazy" (Yiddish *foyl*) indicts those who have given up hope, too weak of spirit to respond to the call of the angel of life. An irony lurks behind Yehoash's word: *foyln* as a verb means "to rot."

The Feet of the Messenger

In 1914 a second journey took Yehoash to the holy land to study Arabic and to "saturate himself with the spirit of ancient Israel in order to devote the remainder of his life to a translation of the Old Testament" (Madison 1968, 166). The record of that journey, entitled in Yiddish *From New York to Rehobot and Back*, was published in an abbreviated English translation by Isaac Goldberg in 1923 as *The Feet of the Messenger*, the version cited here. The title and epigram are adapted from Isaiah 52:7: "How beautiful upon the mountains are the feet of the messenger" who, as the verse continues, "brings good news." Thinking he will resettle in the holy land (and having no way of knowing at the start that the outbreak of World War I will force him to return to America), Yehoash begins the memoir with an elegy to his "adopted home" in Colorado: "I had grown to love her prairies and her mountains, her lakes and her vast spaces, her gigantic pioneer spirit, her breadth and her freedom" (1923, 12). Anticipating his departure, the traveler now looks forward (in an introductory chapter called "Redemption") to a "new spring, a new youth, with new, firm beliefs" (9). Once in the holy land, he reads Theodor Herzl's *Judenstaat*, Zionism's founding declaration, and savors the "odor of the Eretz Yisroel soil [that] rises from his printed words—the unity and the vigor, the healing restorative power of that soul" (188). Yet he describes the urge to make his *aliyah* in what may be an unconsciously ambiguous metaphor of germination: "In a hidden crevice of the soul a seed had taken root and was quietly, modestly burgeoning" (9). From a seed new life can sprout in the soil of Eretz Yisroel. The soul is invigorated by the restorative power of Herzl's vision, as the health of the body had been restored in the clear air of the Rockies. The "messenger," speaking with the voice of Isaiah as the prophet of "good news," foresees the burgeoning of his transplanted soul as the seed of a story to be writ large in the fulfillment of Herzl's vision of a new Jewish homeland. But in the parlance of the sanatorium, once Koch's germ theory had been accepted as the cause of tuberculosis, the fatal *bacillus* could be said to "seed" itself in the patient.[5] Like an incipient tubercular infection, Yehoash's seed "remained unobserved," yet "in reposeful moments a breath would arise . . . filling the spirit with sorrow and boundless yearning" (9). Here the sorrow of his departure mingles both with the memory of a

5. When pulmonary tuberculosis spread from the lungs to the other organs it was called "miliary tuberculosis," or "disseminated tuberculosis" because of the similarity of a scattering of tiny lesions in the lung visible in an x-ray to millet seeds. In 1883 the president of the American Public Health Association, Dr. Ezra Hunt, riffing off the Parable of the Sower in his presidential address (published in the journal *Public Health* in that year), spoke of the tuberculosis germ as a "seed," arguing that the disease will take root only in those individuals with a weak constitution. If the "infective particle" is sown "in the unfriendly soil of a pure life or pure dwelling place it perishes" (Hunt 1883, 16).

tainted tubercular breath (and the fear of every recovered tubercular that the infection could recur), and the yearning for the odor of the promised land where itinerant the soul could finally put down roots.

The Feet of the Messenger begins with the traveler's reflection on what may have impelled him to undertake the journey from America: "Perhaps the bracing winds of your prairies have awakened the dead generation in my soul. Perhaps the majestic peaks of your snow-capped mountains have urged and heartened me to answer the call" (Yehoash 1923, 12). If Yehoash sets out as Abraham, he ends as Moses. Like the Torah, *The Feet of the Messenger* rises to its conclusion with a vision of Mount Nebo:

> We turn our glances in the direction of the mountains of Moab, which are discernible in the distance. Above them a white mist lazily hovers. On one of these mountains—Mt. Nebo—stood the great leader, and looked down upon the Promised Land, and thought of the people whom he loved more than his own life—the people he had fed and nourished with the blood of his own heart. There he stood and gazed mournfully and lovingly at the land from a distance. For the great Jehovah had said to him: "Get thee up into this mountain of Abarim, unto mount Nebo, which is in the land of Moab, that is over against Jericho; and behold the land of Canaan, which I give unto the children of Israel for a possession . . . For thou shalt see the land afar off; but thou shalt not go thither into the land which I give the children of Israel." (238–39)

Yehoash's trek from New York to Colorado is measured by the distance between the Catskills and the Rockies. Similarly bracketed by two mountains, his journey forward from the sanatorium takes the Jewish tubercular from the land of promise in Colorado to the Promised Land for the tubercular Jew—to the restorative soil where the itinerant can find his roots, and finally take root. Yet the prospect at the end is clouded by a hovering mist. The journey is incomplete. The "boundless yearning" returns as a mournful gaze. Moses was granted a vision of the Promised Land from the mountain top, but there he was to die, forbidden to enter.

For Yehoash's reader, and very likely for Yehoash himself, the moment recalls "The Prophet's Fate" from the 1907 collection (168–69). Headed by an epigraph in God's very words to Moses in Deuteronomy 52—"you shall not enter"—this Yiddish poem speaks in a voice seemingly addressed to the poet as well as to the reader. Every verse begins with the refrain *nit du*: "Not you, who will see the land of Canaan"; "Not you, who turned your gaze to heavens stars on quiet desert nights"; "Not you, in whose breast the lovely dream first grew":

> And would you know your prophet's fate? ——
> To perish in the desert with your final breath,
> The howling of the beasts in the wild,
> The poisoned hiss of desert snakes,
> The hour of death will echo with these sounds.

The poem's baneful desert soundscape, literally that of the Sinai, reverberates with the sounds piercing the quiet of a Colorado night on the high plains in December 1906, the date affixed to the poem: the howl of a coyote, the hiss of the gopher snake. To die in Denver would be to share the prophet's fate but also the biblical grandeur of his vision. In consolation, the poem assures Moses that a successor will complete the journey—one of "clear spirit," one who "drinks in your word, and strengthens himself with it," and who "will accomplish what you only dreamed." In 1906 the fate that awaits "you" is far from clear. You do not know whether you will ever be able to see the Promised Land. Will you die the death of Moses in the desert, your task unfinished and left to others? Or will "you" be the Joshua inspired by Moses's word to carry on? In the poem's word, "you" would then be the *yoresh* of "the prophet's dream"—literally, the heir, but in Yiddish carrying the connotation of father's bequest to a son, the passing on of a tradition and a duty. In 1906 Yehoash had already determined upon his plan for the Yiddish Bible. The journey to Eretz Yisroel in 1914 took Yehoash to the geographical destination foreclosed to Moses. He would then return to New York, strengthened and determined to finish translating the word of Moses. In a

Mosaic irony the translator might have savored, Yehoash brought his life's work to the very brink of completion but died before he could get there.

The Collected Poems

More than the dictionary and the incipient Bible translation, pieces of which would begin to appear in print only years later, the *Collected Poems* of 1907 (from which the examples above are taken) immediately secured Yehoash's reputation as a major Yiddish writer. Its success was due in part to the arrangement of the volume, which grouped the material under headings congenial in turn to all the stakeholders in the enterprise of Yiddish literature: lyric poems, poems based on the Bible and the Talmud, "national" poems, occasional poems, and a section of recent poems all composed (and dated) between December 1905 and February 1907. The more meditative, inward-looking lyrics are tinged with an erotic pantheism. He prays that the world should drink in his soul ("As the earth drinks in / A speck of dew that night has left behind"). These spoke to the aestheticism of *Di Yunge* movement, which, as characterized by Ruth Wisse, sought its inspiration in "artistic beauty" alone, "independent of social, ethical, or national value" (Wisse 1976, 265; quoted in Goldstick 1952, 19). Yehoash's "national" poems, on the other hand, speak to a "love for the folk" as a flower that thrives in adversity (Goldstick 1952, 296) and commemorate a 1905 Russian pogrom in Zhitomir among other calamities. Although some poems were written earlier, those specifically dated between 1905 and 1907 emerge from Yehoash's time in Colorado. This section has a very loose narrative structure bounded on both ends by mortality, beginning with a poem entitled "On the Immigrants' Ship" that focuses on the nighttime death of passenger on route (339), and ending with a meditation on "The Ephemeral" in which the "deep night" swallows up the spark of human life after its one glimmering moment (388).

It is a sad reflection on the fate of Yiddish in America that Yehoash's *Collected Poems* cannot be read in the original by those who have lost the language and would not be read by Jews in the pockets of ultra-orthodoxy where Yiddish can still be heard on the street but who regard reading secular literature in any language a waste of time at best and at worst a temptation to be shunned. As a volume, it is also unavailable to English speakers since it has never been translated in full. To do so is a temptation I must resist at the moment, focusing instead on those aspects of the early poetry rooted (to use Yehoash's word) in his Colorado experience, and ramified in his other work during the period of his recuperation.[6] The argument I have advanced so far is that the dictionary, the nascent Bible translation and the poems of 1907 all grow from a common *shtam*, one of whose branches will grow further in the writer's call to the holy land and his reflections on his experience there in *The Feet of Messenger*. To return to my opening question, then: with his deep commitment to these other projects, not to mention his administrative interest in the sanatorium during a time when we must imagine that his energy was sapped by tuberculosis, what could have impelled Yehoash to undertake yet another major piece of work, and why *Hiawatha*?

Why *Hiawatha*?

Two immediate answers seem obvious, the first more so than the second. Many poets tried their hand at turning the masterpieces of English verse into Yiddish. The intention was at once to make the classics available to Yiddish readers in the service of Americanization, and to demonstrate that Yiddish, sometimes viewed as mere *dzargon* by Hebraists and Americanizers alike, could match the high literary level of English canonical works. Among the most ambitious

6. The most ample collection of Yehoash's verse in English translation is to be found in Harshav and Harshav's *Sing, Stranger* (2006), 79–113. The thirty-six poems included in this anthology were all written after 1910, and appear under the heading "The Lyric Turn"—one aspect only, albeit a major one, of Yehoash's work. The earlier 1907 volume (unmentioned in Harshav and Harshav's headnote on Yehoash) represents in my view the foundation, laid in the Colorado soil over a period of ten crucial years in Yehoash's formation as a writer, of everything that came after.

of such American translators, Berl Lapin (1889–1952) published Shakespeare's sonnets in Yiddish in 1953 ("Shall I compare thee to a summer's day" becomes *Zol ikh farglaykhn dikh tsum zumer-tog?*), as well as translations of Blake, Dickinson and Frost. From other hands would come Yiddish versions of Whitman, Tennyson, and the *Rubbaiyyat of Omar Khayyam*, the last also translated by Yehoash. *Hiawatha* itself had been translated into Russian in 1896 by Ivan Bunin (who in 1933 would be the first Russian writer to win the Nobel Prize for literature), and Longfellow's poem would appear again, three years after Yehoash's Yiddish version, in Shaul Tchernichovsky's Hebrew translation of 1913. Yehoash, it would appear, was part of a *Hiawatha* boomlet in the translation business. I've already noted that Yehoash's translation of Byron's "The Wild Gazelle" at the age of twenty-one was heralded by Peretz as the entry of "our Byron" onto the literary scene. Set in "Judah's hills" and contrasting the rootedness of the palm trees with "Israel's scattered race," Byron's poem concludes:

> But we must wander witheringly,
> In other lands to die;
> And where our fathers' ashes be,
> Our own can never lie [.] (1827, 64)

For Yehoash, rendering these lines into Yiddish represents not only an homage to Byron but an adaption into Yiddish of the fundamental themes of immigrant writing, and of Yehoash's later poetry. He would also try his hand at faux-exotic poems such as a "Prayer to Buddha" (Goldstick 1952, 72), "Yang-Ze-Fu," about a Chinese empress (Chametzky et al. 2001, 143), "Fun Yen," the "monk of the mountains" (Harshav and Harshav 2006, 107–08)—exercises in what might be called fictional translation as part of an effort "to expand the cultural range of Yiddish literature" (Chametzky et al., 140). Overall, Yehoash "translated hundreds of works from many languages (English, Russian, German, Hebrew, French, Arabic) into Yiddish," including his "masterful Yiddish rendering of Longfellow's *Hiawatha*" (Harshav and Harshav, 79).

To master Longfellow was not only to match the technical achievement of his verse in another language over the long haul of Yehoash's *Dos Lied fun Hayavata*. It was also to emulate the literary grandee widely praised in his lifetime as the most popular and successful, if not the greatest, American poet. By 1910, the year of Yehoash's *Hayavata*, Longfellow (along with his friend and admirer John Greenleaf Whittier) had not yet fallen from the pinnacle of American letters, to be replaced in twentieth-century critical opinion by Emily Dickinson and Walt Whitman. Would publishing a Yiddish *Hayavata* qualify the translator as "our Longfellow," just as he had earlier been proclaimed "our Byron"? As a reader of Longfellow, furthermore, Yehoash would be familiar with one of the master's most celebrated poems, "The Jewish Cemetery at Newport." Here he would find Longfellow's elegy for an extinguished race whose "very names recorded here are strange" (1922, 335–37, l. 13). The only vestige of the Jews' once-thriving presence in Newport is to be found in "these sepulchral stones, so old and brown," that seem "like tablets of the Law, thrown down / And broken by Moses at the mountain's base" (ll. 12–15). The lament in Longfellow's final stanza for "dead nations" that "never rise again" (l. 60) could befit Hiawatha's people as well as the Jews of Newport. The dead, however, are "not neglected; for a hand unseen, / . . . Still keeps their graves and their remembrance green" (ll. 26–28), We might say there are four hands at work in the unseen collaboration between Longfellow and Yehoash: the unseen caretaker's hand in the Jewish cemetery; the Christian poet's hand in preserving the memory of the dead beneath the sepulchral stones in "The Jewish Cemetery"; his hand again, in commemorating the Native American past in *The Song of Hiawatha*; and the hand of Yehoash, keeping the remembrance of the dead Christian poet green by translating his *Song* into a new (albeit very old) language for the benefit of a greenhorn readership unschooled in Longfellow and unfamiliar with the mythic American past *Hiawatha* purports to "keep."

If the prospect of becoming "our" Longfellow drew Yehoash to *Hiawatha* in the first place, the second reason for his interest in the project may simply have been that his sojourn to Colorado brought him into contact with Native Americans for the first time. Although this claim cannot be documented in the case of Yehoash, it stands as a reasonable conjecture. People living in Colorado at the beginning of the twentieth century knew they were in Indian Territory. As we have seen, lungers in Colorado Springs knew that "the Manatou here dwelt in days gone by." The "Meeker Massacre" of 1879—when the Utes killed eleven people, including the Indian Agent Nathaniel Meeker, in reprisal for the seizure of their lands and the attempt to Americanize them as peaceful Christian farmers—was still a living memory. (After the "massacre," a prominent Jewish railroad builder and newspaper publisher named Otto Mears was appointed to lead an Indian delegation to Washington for treaty negotiations.) The tubercular Yiddish poet Rueben Ludwig (1895–1926), who died while chasing the cure in the American southwest, wrote a series of poems, angry and elegiac by turn, about the destruction of a once-great race at the hands of "those who are rich in fire water" and came "with crosses on their chests": "Sleep, brown warriors, at the edge of the passing realms" (Cooperman 1967, 294, 295). Ludwig's *Collected Poems* were published in 1927 and would surely have been familiar to Yehoash. As late as the 1960s bands of Native Americans performing their "traditional" war dances or rain dances in full regalia (and expecting a modest contribution for their trouble) were a common attraction. For many, including JCRS patients, the highlight of a day trip from the Denver area to Colorado Springs or to Pueblo was to see the Indians who staged hourly performances in good weather and then obligingly posed for photographs. Souvenir tomahawks and feathered headdresses could always be purchased at nearby shops. The annual Denver "March Powwow," featuring competitions in drumming and dance, still fills the city coliseum today.

The JCRS archive contains three photographs of groups of Indian entertainers, costumed in feathers, beaded skirts, moccasins and ankle bells on the grounds of the sanatorium. In one image a dozen or so dancers form a semicircle in the background while two small white children in the center are given the privilege of inspecting the performers' ceremonial drum close up. In another, the entire cast of the "world-famous Cheyenne Rodeo," cowboys and Indians together, is assembled for a group picture on the occasion of their special performance at the sanatorium in 1940. The third, a candid shot, shows a smaller cluster of performers lounging on the grass, evidently taking a break before or after their performance (figure 5).

One is smoking a cigarette. A small boy looks on in fascination, but patients can be seen strolling or chatting in the background, suggesting that the presence of the troupe is not an extraordinary sight. These photographs are found in the file of a patient named Leon Newman, who was under care at the JCRS from the late thirties, long after Yehoash's departure. But if there is room to speculate, one can wonder what a Lithuanian Jewish intellectual, newly transplanted from the Lower East Side to the no longer quite "wild" west at the foot of the Rockies, might have made of these strange people?

In a reminiscence of his childhood in Chernowitz, the distinguished Yiddish scholar Mordkhe Schaechter (1927–2007) recalls the impression made on boys his age by the "western" novels of the German writer Karl May (1842–1912), whose works were translated into many languages, including Yiddish. There was the Apache chief Winnetou and the cowboy Old Shatterhand, enemies at first but then comrades (the Indian calls the cowboy "my brother") who go on many adventures together. Schaechter's memoir reproduces the cover illustration of May's *Der Fürst der Bleichgesichter* (The Prince of the Palefaces) showing the pair of stalwart frontier comrades riding side by side in what may be taken as the Teutonic avatar of the Lone Ranger and his faithful Indian companion. What strikes the child Schaechter most forcibly, however, is the account he sees in May of the way in which the Indians were "exploited and murdered and exterminated"—the victims of a new world holocaust. He resolves to travel to America to save them from their fate, only to realize in time that the expedition would be in vain. But in later life Schaechter would see a "thread" connecting his early concern for the plight of the Indians with his sympathy for all oppressed minorities (including

5. "Indian Entertainment": Native Americans taking a break from their performance on the grounds of the JCRS. Photograph courtesy of Beck Archives, Special Collections, CJS and University Libraries, University of Denver.

Palestinians and orthodox Jewish women under the thumb of their sexist husbands).[7]

A similar thread connects the Jews to Yehoash's Indians. In the Colorado of the early 1900s it would be clear to newly arrived Jewish lungers, whether influenced by Karl May or not, that the real Native Americans they encountered had little of the mythic grandeur of the fictional Winnetou. Rather, the Indians were the remnant of a dispossessed *volk*, reduced to playing at being the fierce

7. Schaechter's memoir (Yiddish) appears as a commemoration of his death, in the Fall 2007 edition of the magazine *Oyfn Shvel* of which he was a long-time editor. I translate from the section entitled "Indians," 45–46. On Jews and Indians, see also Rubenstein, *Members of the Tribe*, especially chapter 2. In her Epilogue, Rubenstein quotes a Rabbi who had participated in a "spiritual gathering" with the Navajo in the 1990s as having "long sensed a Profound weave of connection between Native Americans and Jewish people": both "tribes" were "driven into exile," and driven from their "ancestral home with genocidal force" (1910, 179).

and proud people they no longer were, re-enacting rituals emptied of their spiritual core, and dependent on the kindness of strangers for their sustenance. What Yehoash made of these strange people was his *Hayavata*, a work of cross-cultural encounter and imaginative identification that would channel Longfellow in order to evoke the powerful myths and the tragic history that lay behind these woebegotten performances. The bond is sealed by putting Yiddish into the mouths of the Indians' aboriginal forbears.

Zhitlovsky's Introduction

Yehoash's translation begins with an introduction by the notable Yiddishist Chaim Zhitlovsky (1865–1943). Concerned with far more than providing an entrée to the poem, Zhitlovsky uses the occasion to develop a substantial essay (in Yiddish) touching on all the controversies, political, religious, and linguistic, swirling around the status of Yiddish in 1910. As an opponent of Zionism, a polemical secularist, and a critic of the doctrinaire pieties of socialism, Zhitlovsky was at the center of these controversies. As a socialist revolutionary in the Russia of his youth, he first believed that the fulfillment of the promises of *Haskalah* for the Jews lay in assimilation, patriotism, and the adoption of the most enlightened values of European culture. "Judaism," for him was to be a religion as universal as Christianity and not the property of any one people. Shaken by the waves of pogroms that swept eastern Europe, however, Zhitlovsky now argued that Jews are after all distinctively a "Jewish people" bound together not by any particular ideology or religious practice, but by *Yiddish*. In 1908 he was one of the prime movers behind the Czernowitz Conference, which would proclaim Yiddish as the "national" language of the Jews. Zhitlovsky would remain faithful to this secular gospel. As late as 1939 he would write: "Today, any Jew who lives with his people in the Yiddish language sphere, whether he believes in the Jewish religion or whether he is an atheist, belongs to the Jewish people" (Zhitlovsky 1939). The atheist who (merely) appreciated the Bible for its poetical beauty and its ethical teachings could count himself as good a Jew as any. In light of Zhitlovsky's enthusiasm for the Yiddish *Hayavata*, we might well feel that Jews, along with all of humanity, should celebrate the simple, human legends of the Native Americans. If the Bible of the Jews is to be read as poetry, then the poetry of the Indians—who have no bible, but whose "Song" is preserved by Longfellow—could be read as a kind of sacred scripture.

When Zhitlovsky finally turns to the poem some twenty pages into his introductory essay, he is moved to declare at the outset that if he had to name a poem "more necessary to Yiddish literature at the present time than any other," he would be hard pressed to find a better example than Yehoash's *Hayavata* (1910, xxi). Why so? His answer is worth quoting in detail (xxii–iv):

> What we, city-and-shtetl folk, lack is nature and the love of her. Our spiritual treasury is wanting, or else those voices do not strongly enough give expression to forest and field, mountain and water. We lack the "scent of the outdoors" so richly infused in Longfellow's poetry.
>
> However, what we also lack (with all due respect) is the ability to enter into the lives of another [or a "strange"] people, not only in an intellectual sense but with feeling and imagination. In our own minds, we are the cosmopolites of the world. In our emotional lives however, our sorrows and anguish have so narrowed our spirit that we have long forgotten to "love a stranger so that you can understand his spirit." . . . We have stopped trying to understand the spirit of non-Jews, and our whole atmosphere is filled with so much chauvinism and clamorous hatred among Jews that there is hardly any air to breath, hatred not only between progressive-nationalists but among those who would never let the cry "Workers of the world rise up" pass their lips. . . . This is not due to a lack of theoretical education, rather to a rawness of feeling that cannot be refined by theory and moralizing, but only through the general [common] poetry of humanity. The poetry of other peoples teaches us sympathy with others, with their joys and

> sorrows. In this respect Longfellow's *Hiawatha* is one of the most worthwhile things in European [!] literature. *Hiawatha* is actually a collection of legends that the wild Indians of North America have created. These legends are in part nature myths—supernatural tales explaining one or another natural appearance. But in part they are also cultural myths, expressing the wonders that primitive minds experience in their own social life, and their understanding and dreams.
>
> [. . .]
>
> Longfellow has clustered all these legends around the central figure of the Indian epic, the mythical hero "Hiawatha." Hiawatha is moreover not an individual hero but the entire Indian people, a personification of all the finest traits of their character and their lives. He is the ideal of the people that reflects everything they hold holy and dear.
>
> [. . .]
>
> Entering into the psychology of the whole Indian people, sympathizing with their troubles and suffering, as these are in the end the same troubles and suffering that afflict all people everywhere: Such feelings begin to make national differences disappear, the enmity between the national "I" and the national "you." There arises instead a feeling of solidarity that in the end will bring all mankind together in brotherly family . . . and help to unite all peoples in order to achieve the common progress of all humanity.
>
> In the struggle for an authentic national existence, in the enmity between the politician and the cosmopolite, we often forget the demands of brotherly love among peoples, the spirit of all our progressive beliefs. . . . Works like *Hiawatha* refresh this very spirit with their pure "humanism." the noble love for people, which in Longfellow is so harmoniously blended with a love of nature.

Zhitlovsky poses an opposition, only then to urge a reconciliation, between the "cosmopolite" and the "primitive." This is not to be achieved by Longfellow's Indians becoming more theoretically sophisticated, but rather by Jews tapping sympathetically into the

Indians' deep well of feeling and imagination, of a love for nature and a "noble" love for people. The spirit of our *volk*—deracinated and ideologically overheated polemicists that we have become—will be refreshed by our reestablishing a brotherly bond with this unsophisticated, but for that reason all the more poetic, *fremde volk*: this "strange" or "other" people to whose rich cultural myths and legends *Hiawatha* gives us access. Zhitlovsky is not alone in believing that *Hiawatha* is an anthropological transcript of Native American mythology, in effect the Indians' Bible. Stripped of their supernaturalism, our own Jewish "legends," such as that of the Passover, may be understood as part of a universal legendary substrate upon which divisive national differences can be reconciled. Our familiarity with the Indian mind—our embracing the Indian other as part of the human family—will have two benefits for the Jews, as individuals and as a "nation" (it being left unclear just what benefits may accrue to the Indians thereby). As a form of therapy, entering into the "psychology" of the primitive will heal the breach between mind and spirit, between thought and feeling, and between culture and nature, thus restoring what in other terms might be thought of as the recuperation of an Eliotic "unified sensibility." Consequently, it would seem that reading *Hiawatha* will be like taking a breath of fresh air, dispelling the stifling atmosphere that hangs over the battlefield of Jewish cultural politics and making us all friends again. Here the Indian polity serves as an example of what might be possible for us. Divided into many tribes from every region of America, Longfellow's Indians nevertheless form one happy family. Hiawatha himself is no "individual" hero but rather, like Moses, the "ideal of the people," a symbol of unity that puts us to shame at a moment when our nation is fractured into competing tribes called the Zionists, the Anti-Zionists, the orthodox Marxists, the Progressive Socialists, the Religionists, and the Secularists, all at each other's throat and all worshipping their own false gods. What's good for the Indians is good for the Jews. A Yiddish-speaking Hiawatha—an amalgam we might call a Yindian or an Indijew—is the literary avatar for the possibility of individual integrity and social unity.

The most recent—and, indeed, to my knowledge the only—discussion of Yehoash's poem in English-language criticism is to be found in Alan Trachtenberg's *Shades of Hiawatha* (2004), where the motives involved in the translation are woven into a broader narrative about the image of the Indian in the formation of American culture between 1880 and 1930. My own reading comports with his (in a chapter entitled "Yiddish Hiawatha") insofar as we both note the main themes of the Zhitlovsky preface: Zhitlovsky's Anti-Zionism, his secular faith in Yiddish as a means of creating "a national culture in diaspora, without a state or territory and with an increasingly tenuous relation to Judaism," his belief, shared with other advocates of Yiddish, that literary translation satisfied "the double desire for an intimacy with gentile culture and for refinement and the preservation of Yiddish as legitimate literary language," and (here quoting Zhitlovsky himself from a separate essay on the value of translation) his conviction that "a people achieves itself by harmonizing its 'yearning for its own unique culture with a connection to the general human progress'" (Trachtenberg 2004, 150, 149, 151). Trachtenberg's subtitle, *Staging Indians, Making Americans*, aptly describes the kind of Native American theatrics on display at the JCRS, but he does not make the connection. Indeed, he passes over Yehoash's years in Colorado without comment, makes no mention of the dictionary, and only notes that a volume of Yehoash's poetry appeared in 1907 (but states incorrectly that the Bible translation was begun in the "early 1920s" [153]). While Trachtenberg's view is panoramic, mine focuses on the immediate circumstances, literary and geographical, that gave rise to Yehoash's *Hiawatha*. Finally more interested in Zhitlovsky than in Yehoash, Trachtenberg has little to say about the content of the translation itself apart from the casual observation that the question-and-answer format the first two stanzas of Longfellow's poem ("Should you ask me, whence these stories . . . I should answer") sounds in Yiddish "more like a Talmudic conversation than a rhetorical pattern of English poetry" (156).

Trachtenberg does, however, point to a blind spot in Zhitlovsky, noting that the introduction to *Hayavata* "buries everything implied by the encounter (by means of translation) between diasporic Jewish yearnings for a homeland (translated into a love of Yiddish) and the dispossession of Indians, which also lies buried and unmentioned by Longfellow, except obliquely in the final cantos" (157). How much Zhitlovsky knew (or cared) about the dispossession of Indians must remain an open question. His regarding Longfellow as a *European* writer, and Yehoash's translation in turn as a contribution to European literature in the first instance, and then to a worldwide Yiddish readership in the second, virtually factors out of his account any engagement with the issues of real Indians. Paramount for Zhitlovsky is the efficacy of the translation for the Jews. What Trachtenberg sees as at stake for Yehoash—"the credibility of Yiddish as a medium of access to the inner life of the American imagination" (159)—was of less concern to Zhitlovsky than the potency of Yiddish as a means of enriching the imagination of Jewish readers and of forging a definitionally "Jewish" bond of solidarity among them. For this purpose, the translation of any prestigious work would serve; it just happens that Longfellow writes about Indians. There is no record of any understanding between Yehoash and Zhitlovsky as to how the latter would come to write the introduction. We must assume that Yehoash approved of it, perhaps in large part because Zhitlovsky, as a prominent figure in Yiddish circles, would confer something of his own scholarly authority on the publication. In any case Yehoash and Zhitlovsky must be separated if the translation is to be examined on its own terms. Thus the question remains, put simply: How in the body of the translation itself, and not in Zhitlovsky's self-serving preface, are we to understand the connection between Jews and Indians, who, thanks to Yehoash, have acquired a wonderful fluency in Yiddish?

Indians and Jews

Zhitlovsky's distinction between (the fantasy of) a happy Indian family and the dysfunctional family of the Jews belies not only the realities of Native American history but the similarities between Jews and Indians in the rhetoric of the day. When the tidal wave of immigrants from Italy and Eastern Europe, the latter almost all Jews, rose to its greatest height at the turn of the century, Francis A. Walker, the director of the 1890 census and formerly commissioner of Indian affairs, raised the alarm in the pages of *The Atlantic Monthly*, warning in 1896 that America would be engulfed by "vast throngs of ignorant and brutalized peasantry" unless restrictions on immigration were put in place (Walker 1896, 822). At the same time, writes Trachtenberg, "Yankee blue bloods and others watched with alarm the increase of 'undesirable' groups—'races,' wrote the patrician Massachusetts Senator Henry Cabot Lodge in 1891, 'most alien to the body of the American people'" (2004, 99). "Aliens" both, the "races" of the Native Americans and the Jews posed an equal threat to the "native" integrity, the genetic purity, and not least the Christianity, of true Americans in the decade of Yehoash's *Hayavata*. For just at the moment when the Indians were finally dispossessed of their lands by treaty or by force, depleted in their numbers, and their remnant moved farther and farther west to distant reservations, suddenly a new and even more insidious alien threat loomed over the horizon from the east.

As Lodge's comment insinuates, the eastern threat to the American "body" was not merely metaphorical. Any one of a long list of infectious diseases—trichinosis, typhus, above all tuberculosis—diagnosed in a cursory physical examination at America's ports of entry could bar the golden door to a would-be immigrant. If such a person were to slip through, he would likely end up in some festering tenement district whose unsanitary conditions, combined with the ignorance of the inhabitants about basic hygiene, would prove a grave menace to public health. Indians, too, when they were not mythologized as the sturdy children of nature, were thought to be disease-ridden—as, indeed were the Navahos of Arizona, Colorado and New Mexico, among whom tuberculosis was endemic, and whose susceptibility to disease was similarly thought to stem from their filthy and primitive way of life.[8] For tubercular Jews in their

8. In 1852 the U.S. government subsidized fifteen western hospitals and sanatoriums, most of them facing bankruptcy when the numbers of Anglo TB patients

hundreds and thousands between 1890 and 1950, the journey to the promised land in America led only to a second dislocation, now from their way stations (and from their families) in the cities of the east, chasing the cure across the American desert to institutions whose distant historical origins lay in the leper colony and the plague hospital. There the Jews might form a new community centered around the TB sanitarium—a community of "lungers" all sharing the same stigma and relying on their mutual support to keep up their spirits if not restore their health. For family members left behind, "Colorado" was more likely to signify some place in the wilderness where Yankel was sent to die; marriages failed when wives or husbands refused to follow their spouses, who might then find consolation in the arms of a "cousin" in the next ward. Such was the (largely irrational) fear of contamination that in the aptly named "Golden Hill" Jewish cemetery up the road from the JCRS, a special section was set aside for those who had died of consumption (most notably the Yiddish poet Dovid Edelshtat), apparently to protect the non-tubercular dead. Against whatever was thought to imperil its well-being, the "native" American "community" sought to "immunize" itself, to borrow Roberto Esposito's sense of "immunity," a term that in his reading of biopolitical thought seeks to straddle the gap between the biological and the political (2008, 45–47). Different in tactics but alike in their ideological motivation, the attempts to establish a cordon sanitaire on America's eastern frontier and the conclusive stage

waned, in return for their "willingness to administer to the medical needs of hundreds of tuberculous Navahos" (McKay 1983, 138). As we have seen, among these institutions was the elite private Cragmor Sanatorium in Colorado Springs, which in its golden age had hosted such distinguished patients as the newspaper heiress Constance Pulitzer, but which now could keep its doors open only by admitting (and attempting to civilize) the Navaho, many of whom, according to the local newspaper, "have never sat in a chair or eaten from a table" ("Navaho Patients Learn How to Raise Living Standards," *Colorado Springs Gazette Telegraph*, March 2, 1958, 1). The same article estimated that TB "strikes one out of every three Navaho families."

of the Indians' expulsion to the western frontier stand as historically overlapping programs of cultural immunization. Thus, in ways Zhitlovsky could not imagine from his "European" perspective, Indians and immigrant Yiddish-speaking Jews were already bound together in Yehoash's America. Both were *fremde*, alien races whose language, religion, and customs were not those of Henry Cabot Lodge. Both represented a threat to "true" Americans. Both were uprooted from their places of origin and sent on a trek across land or water—although, as it happened, toward a better life ultimately for the Jews, but a dead end for the Native Americans.

Hayavata

When he set about his translation on the grounds of the JCRS, Yehoash found himself surrounded by the landscape that Longfellow, at his Cambridge writing desk, could only imagine for his legendary Indians in "the far-off Rockies"—the word "mountain" appears thirty-one times in *Hiawatha*, and the word "prairie" or "prairies" thirty-three. Conjuring a scene reminiscent of that in "The Jewish Cemetery at Newport," Longfellow introduces his *Hiawatha* by asking us to "Pause by some neglected graveyard," now an Indian burial ground, and to "Read this Song of Hiawatha" as if the entire poem to follow—as well as the "tender pathos" we will feel for the passing of an ancient race—were legible in the "half-effaced inscription" on a tombstone:

> Ye, who sometimes, in your rambles
> Through the green lanes of the country,
> Where the tangled barberry-bushes
> Hang their tufts of crimson berries
> Over stone walls gray with mosses,
> Pause by some neglected graveyard,
> For a while to muse, and ponder
> On a half-effaced inscription,
> Written with little skill of song-craft,
> Homely phrases, but each letter

Full of hope and yet of heart-break,
Full of all the tender pathos
Of the Here and the Hereafter;
Stay and read this rude inscription,
Read this Song of Hiawatha! (1855, 8–9)

In his rendering of this passage (1910, 8), as he does throughout Longfellow's poem, Yehoash carefully observes the line breaks of the English original and marches to the beat of Longfellow's distinctive trochaic tetrameters, arguably a more difficult feat in Yiddish than in English. In this respect Yehoash's Yiddish—such is the song-craft of the translator—functions as a sort of transparent overlay, allowing the reader to see (and, in the rhythm, hear) the English beneath it. All the more discordant, then, is Yehoash's use of three resonant Hebrew words imported into Yiddish: *bays oylom* ("cemetery," literally "eternal house") for Longfellow's "graveyard" in the fifth line above; *matseyve* ("gravestone") for Longfellow's "rude inscription" in the next-to-last line of the passage; and most significant because it represents a departure from Longfellow's "half-effaced inscription" in the eighth line, "*po-nikbar*" ("here lies," literally "here [is] entombed") in quotation marks. Yiddish does offer a literal translation for "inscription" as *oyfshrift*, an obvious choice. But just here Yehoash chooses to emend the line by replacing Longfellow's gesture toward an inscription with the very phrase that we would expect to find on the gravestone of a Jew. This introductory scene of reading constructs the text it lays before us as a kind of palimpsest. *Hiawatha*, a book of ancient Indian legends "half-effaced" by time, is to be written over, in both senses of the word, as the Yiddish *Hayavata*.

This kinship of the Indians and the Jews is more than implicit in key passages of Longfellow's poem. When Gitche Manito, the "creator of the nations," chides the assembled Indian tribes for their "wranglings and dissensions," we can overhear the voice of a Zhitlovsky trying to bring order to some international congress of bickering Jews:

I am weary of your quarrels,
Weary of your wars and bloodshed,
Weary of your prayers for vengeance,
Of your wranglings and dissensions;
All your strength is in your union,
All your danger is in discord;
Therefore be at peace henceforward,
And as brothers live together. (1855, 16–17)

Gitche Manito then announces that he “will send a prophet to you”:

A Deliverer of the nations,
Who shall guide you and shall teach you,
Who shall toil and suffer with you.
If you listen to his counsels,
You will multiply and prosper;
If his warnings pass unheeded,
You will fade away and perish! (17)

The creator’s immediate audience will perhaps fathom that the promised deliverer will be a great leader like Hiawatha. Longfellow’s Christian reader may see in this figure a type of Christ, some glimmer of a deliverance more profound than any Indian creator could bring about. For the word “prophet,” however, Yehoash here (14) prefers the biblical *novi* to the closer Yiddish cognate *profet* (used elsewhere, e.g., 267). Yehoash’s Jewish over-reader will make a different connection: not to the prophetic Hiawatha but to Elijah the Prophet—*Elyohu ha-novi*—whose name is invoked during the Passover seder, and whose hoped-for return will usher in an era of peace to complete the narrative of deliverance begun with the Exodus.

Late in poem, Hiawatha has a most rare vision confirming the report that the white men have arrived. He urges his brethren to welcome them because “The Great Spirit, the Creator, / Sends them hither on his errand. Nevertheless Hiawatha’s prophetic dream of his people’s future ends in a “darker, drearier vision”:

> I beheld our nation scattered,
> All forgetful of my counsels,
> Weakened, warring with each other:
> Saw the remnants of our people
> Sweeping westward, wild and woful,
> Like the cloud-rack of a tempest,
> Like the withered leaves of Autumn! (1855, 283)

Here lies something more than an oblique prophecy of the Indians' dispossession. What remains unmentioned is not the prospect of their dreary future, but rather the historical calamities that will bring it about: their destiny, as envisioned here, will be sealed not by the ruthless western sweep of white America across their homelands, but by inter-tribal warfare among a people already debilitated because they have forgotten the counsels of their mythical prophet. If *Hiawatha* blames the victims, *Hayavata* holds the mirror up to the Jews—like the Indians a "nation scattered," interminably "warring with each other" in the newspapers, meeting halls and coffee shops, the weakened remnant of a once-cohesive spiritual community. But was it ever otherwise? Yehoash's ultimately secular attempt to reconstitute that community on the basis of Yiddish, his intention to re-sacralize Yiddish by foregrounding its Hebrew component in the dictionary, even his commitment to making the Bible legible again for people who no longer had the benefit of a traditional religious education, leaves unspoken the thought reflected in the passage above. Can it be that the Jews' faith in, or at least their nostalgia for, a time when the "nation" was united under a "creator," a "deliverer," a "*novi*," is nothing more than the vestige of a primitive mythology? And if the Jews' origin story is no more credible than the poetic fantasy of an arm-chair cultural anthropologist, might they not also "fade away and perish," leaving not a rack behind?

In the final chapter, with Hiawatha preparing to depart "To the Land of the Hereafter," his role as the prophet will now be filled by the "Black-Robe chief," a Christian priest just off the boat. I cite the newcomer's "message to the people" from *Hiawatha*, followed by the corresponding passage translated from *Hayavata* in order to illustrate Yehoash's most radical and telling departure from Longfellow's poem:

Longfellow:
  Then the Black-Robe chief, the Prophet,
Told his message to the people,
Told the purport of his mission,
Told them of the Virgin Mary,
And her blessed Son, the Saviour,
How in distant lands and ages
He had lived on earth as we do;
How he fasted, prayed, and labored;
How the Jews, the tribe accursed,
Mocked him, scourged him, crucified him;
How he rose from where they laid him,
Walked again with his disciples,
And ascended into heaven.

  And the chiefs made answer, saying:
"We have listened to your message,
We have heard your words of wisdom,
We will think on what you tell us.
It is well for us, O brothers,
That you come so far to see us!"
  Then they rose up and departed
Each one homeward to his wigwam,
To the young men and the women
Told the story of the strangers
Whom the Master of Life had sent them
From the shining land of Wabun. (1855, 290–91)

Yehoash:
Then did the prophet, the "black robe,"
Explain his mission to the people,
The purpose of his coming.

And then said the chiefs:
"We have heard your mission,
"Heard the words of wisdom,
"Well will we think on them.
"It's well for us, dear brothers,
"That you have come from far to see us."

Everyone then rose up,
And went home to his wigwam,
And told his wife and children
The story of the strangers [*fremde*]
Whom the lord of life had sent them
From the shining land of Voban. (1910, 267)

In both versions the chiefs' response to the black-robed prophet is polite but guarded. They welcome the newcomer and appear eager to tell their wives and children the story. The Jews themselves, as *fremde* of a different tribe, might wish for the same warm hospitality from the "native" Americans. With Hiawatha preparing for his final voyage, this new prophet seems destined to take his place. For Longfellow's reader, Hiawatha's endorsement of his Christian successor seems to be underwritten by a familiar providentialist script that recasts the Indian prophet as an honorary Old Testament Jew, a latter-day Elijah pointing the way to the coming of the savior.

But as to the substance of the message, the "words of wisdom" it seems to contain, in both versions the chiefs agree only to think the matter over. These new "brothers"—in Yehoash, these "*dear*" brothers—are strangers after all. Indians, New England Brahmins and (*pace Zhitlovsky*) Jews all know that it's only prudent to regard *di fremde* with some suspicion. Although they recognize the authority of prophets, Longfellow's chiefs may yet harbor some unspoken premonition about the future of their people if they should prove too eager to walk with the disciples of this new savior. In the story told by Longfellow's black-robed prophet, "the Jews" are given a cameo role, but a crucial one, as the "tribe accursed" that killed the Virgin Mary's blessed son. It is unlikely that Longfellow endorses this (Jesuit?) calumny—moved as he was by the Jewish graveyard in Newport to wonder what "burst of Christian hate," what "persecution, merciless and blind" (ll. 29–30) drove the Jews from their homelands. Although descended from a Puritan strain through his mother, Longfellow is known to have been more benevolent and less doctrinaire in his faith than were his New England forbears. He was influenced by the Unitarianism of William Henry Channing, a family friend, who wrote that Longfellow "did not belong to any one sect but rather to the community of those free minds who loved the truth." But whatever distance Longfellow may have wanted to put between himself and his black-robed prophet, Longfellow's text triangulates Indians, Christians, and Jews so as to imply that the brotherhood of the first two tribes is to be confirmed by their rejection of the third. Intended or not, the passage also hints at the bitter irony awaiting the future of the Indians, who will end up, like the Jews, as the "tribe accursed" by their dear brothers in Christ.

So what is a Yiddish translator to make of all this? Here as nowhere else in the poem Yehoash finds the scissors mightier than the pen: he simply cuts the ten lines recounting the message of the black-robe prophet and moves directly into the response of the chiefs. *They* have heard the "words of wisdom," but *we* have not. Of course Yehoash's reader will have little difficulty in surmising what the priest is likely to have said in his inaugural address on American soil. It will be the same message delivered by priests and Czarist agitators throughout the Pale of Settlement, and its purport in those regions is to instigate violence against the Jews. Yehoash's motives for eliding these ten lines remain a matter for speculation. Does he not wish to inflict them on the reader? Does he want to sanitize the poem for the sake of Longfellow's prestige as the sort of classical author Yiddish speakers should admire? Would including the details of such a virulent message make it more difficult for Zhitlovsky to recommend the poem as providing an occasion for the reader "to understand the spirit of non-Jews"? Perhaps they would understand that spirit all too well. The priest's synopsis of a Christology that hinges on the malevolence of the Jews would surely dampen the spirit of a secular

Yiddishist who would like to believe—and even more, would like enlightened Christians to believe—that the Jewish "religion" is not integral to being a Jew, and that religious differences should not stand in the way of universal brotherhood. The literal effect of Yehoash's lacuna is to silence the priest by excising the anti-Semitic tumor in the heart of his message. More charitably, the omission leaves open the possibility—more a fond hope or a counterfactual surmise—that this prophet, or some other, sent by the "lord of life" from the "shining land" might actually bring the words of an enlightened Christian wisdom to the new world.

My attempt in this discussion of Yehoash has been to stitch together the varied pieces of his life's work—the dictionary, the poetry, the Yiddish Bible, the travel writing, the translation of *Hiawatha*—if not into a seamless literary biography, then at least into a critical narrative arguing that these disparate projects are of a piece. The persistent themes of Yehaosh's writing—displacement, wandering, the thinning out of religious tradition, internal cleavages in the *folk*, the status of Hebrew and Yiddish, and the consequently vexed question of what it means to be a Jew in a Christian world—engage the common concerns of Yiddish writers in the diaspora.[9] These themes are woven into an ongoing spiritual autobiography that can be read through the different genres of Yehoash's life projects. Insofar as the life retraces the steps of the Israelites through exile from the father's house in search of the promised land, first in Colorado and then, answering the call, in Eretz Yisroel where he shares Moses's vision from the top of the mountain, this patchwork autobiography comports with Augustine's understanding of the "part" the writer plays in his own life. In a passage near the end of the *Confessions* Augustine compares the reading of scripture with the "life of an individual

9. According to one definition, a Jew is somebody who keeps asking what it means to be a Jew. The tense relation between Jews and non-Jews is the point of a joke that had already grown a long beard in Yehoash's day: Two Jews face a firing squad. One of them asks the captain of the guard for a blindfold. The other turns to his companion and whispers, "Abe, don't make trouble."

person," where "all actions are parts of a whole, and of the total history of 'the sons of men' (Ps. 30:20) in which all human lives are but parts" (1998, 243). In this sense, Yehoash is completing his story as well as that of the Jewish people when, in the end, he devotes his life to translating the Bible into his "own" language. As the narrative of the exodus moves from Mount Sinai to Mount Nebo, Yehoash's moves from his "far-off western home" in the Rockies to the far-off homeland of the Jews, and from imagining himself as the eagle on his "rocky throne," lonely but "anointed," to imagining Moses looking "down upon the Promised Land" from a similar lonely height. After the healing of his body at the JCRS, in Eretz Yisroel Yehoash is moved to feel "the healing restorative power" of Herzl's Zionist vision for the body of the Jewish people. His experience in the sanatorium is, I would thus argue, the singular transformative period of his life, a rebirth from which everything else follows.

3

Leivick and the "Ballad of Denver Sanatorium"

The Idiom of Common Souls

H. Leivick (1888–1962) was admitted to the JCRS in June 1932. With two brief intermissions he remained there until September 1935.[1] Grey and thin when he arrived, his case was diagnosed as "far advanced." His patient record indicates that he left "quiescent" and with a good prognosis. Thus cured, the poet would be granted another quarter century of productive writing and continuing public acclaim until his death. Before his departure, *The Denver Post* ran a valedictory article about the Yiddish poet, playwright, and journalist who was about to return to the greater world after three years in the "little known world of a tuberculosis sanatorium" on the city's western fringe (Radetsky 1935). Few of its local readers will have heard of Leivick, the *Post* assumes, because the "language of his art is a strange thing," not Hebrew but a "hybrid language born in the wanderings of a race," and (in a neat phrase one imagines Leivick must have fed the reporter) a language "expressing the idiom of common souls not of common soil." But "there are millions of persons in Poland, Russia, Germany and Palestine who wait for his phrases

1. Born Leivick Halpern, he signed himself as "H. Leivick" (sometimes appearing in English as "Leyvik") so as to avoid being confused with the famous Yiddish poet Moyshe Leyb Halpern. The two intermissions (from April 18, 1933, to September 6, 1934, and from May 22, 1935, until June 6, 1935) did not result in any lasting improvement in Leivick's health, obliging him to return to the sanatorium.

with all the avidity of the American who once waited for Walt Whitman to phrase the emotional truth of a race." Leivick tells the *Post*, "It is natural that I am not known here. . . . What I write is not for this country. It is not even for the Jews in America. It is for a people far away, a people that remembers, as I remember, a heart and a mind that was purely Jewish." What he wrote during the three years of his recuperation in Denver came in a burst of creative energy to rival that of Yehoash in the previous generation, but these works have not as yet been taken together as a body of work emerging from his experience as a sanatorium patient. Among the major texts of this period, the one closest to the heart and mind of its tubercular author is the "Ballad of Denver Sanatorium" (1934), the culminating poem in Leivick's *Poems from the Garden of Eden*.[2]

As Leivick rode back to New York on a charity train ticket purchased for him by the JCRS, the "millions of persons" who comprised his worldwide audience would need no introduction to the poet of *The Messiah in Chains* (1908), written during Leivick's four years in Czarist prisons, when he was convicted of having joined the Bund, a Jewish social-democratic underground party, and of having distributed incendiary literature on its behalf. Yiddish readers would know him as the author of two inaugural collections of verse (published in 1918 and 1923), and above all as the prolific dramatist whose masterpiece, *The Golem*, had been published in 1921. Leivick's travels in the years following Denver took him beyond New

2. The Yiddish text of the "Ballad" is from the collection *Poems from the Garden of Eden* in *The Complete Works* of 1940, vol. 1, 499–512. The first part of this collection covers the years 1932–1936. The second part includes works from 1937–1940. My translation, here used, appears in "H. Leivick's 'Ballad of the Denver Sanatorium': A Translation," *Rocky Mountain Jewish Historical Notes* (Summer/Fall 1989), 3–9, and is reprinted here in Appendix A. I am grateful to the Rocky Mountain Jewish Historical Society and to its director, Dr. Jeanne Abrams, for permission to make use of this translation, and of some details of my introduction to it in that publication, for the present purpose. One aim of my discussion is to restore this major poem to the canon of Leivick's work, and Leivick criticism, in English.

York to the 1936 P.E.N. conference in Buenos Aires as the representative of Yiddish writers, to the 1937 Jewish World Congress in Paris, and to Palestine. In 1957, a year before he was felled by a paralytic stroke, he went to Israel for the third time, to address a scholarly conference in Jerusalem on the vitality of Yiddish as "the language of the intimate folk spirit" (Madison 1968, 370–71, 379). In 1970, Leyvik House, the Israeli center for Yiddish writing and publication, was established in his honor in Tel Aviv. Among all the writers recently canonized in *Jewish American Literature: A Norton Anthology*, Leivick is "[c]onsidered internationally the greatest Yiddish poet of the mid-twentieth century" (Chametzky et al. 2001, 282).

Leivick's prominence over the long span of his writing life is due in part to his steady productivity and in part to his role in the Yiddish imaginary as "a symbol of redemptive suffering" (Chametzky et al. 2001, 282). He is also a poet for all seasons in the ever-shifting climate of literary movements and rival schools. His work can be political, ethical, biblical, introspective, patriotic, celebratory, anguished, and visionary by turns. He wrote poetic dramas, lyrics, and longer narrative poems, and his verse forms are as protean as his moods—from the clipped, telegraphic style of a poem like "Kabbalists in Safed" ("Half night / In a white fog. / A passage / A street") to the rhapsodic sprawl of his late paean "To America," a land "Sanctified and blessed by the blood of Lincoln's sacrifice / And in the hymns of Walt Whitman" (Harshav and Harshav 1986, 757; Chametzky et al. 2001, 287).[3] Most accounts of Leivick's life tend to focus either

3. Ruth R. Wisse's comments on Leivick (in "*Di Yunge*" [1976]) reflect the poet's protean sensibilities. In the teens the one-time Bundist and social revolutionary announced himself as a devotee of a refined aestheticism: "'We are a sect;' wrote Leivick of the group [the coterie of *Di Yunge*] in its prime, 'we set ourselves apart from everyone, not only from other writers, but from everyone. We want to be separate, our ears cannot tolerate the false sounds, the cheapened literature'" (Wisse 1976, 268). When he "later broke with the privatism of the Yunge to cultivate a more forceful, social, rhetorical voice," he "remained bound to this earlier national motif of passivism and patience" marked by an "eternal longing" (Wisse

on his early struggles and hard-won achievements—his escape from Siberia in 1912, his laboring as a paper hanger in New York, his association with *Di Yunge*, and his writing of *The Golem*—or else on the fruits of his later career as the elder statesman of Yiddish literature, including his anti-Nazi and Holocaust poetry of the forties, the verse drama *In the Days of Job* (1953), and his two final collections of poems, *A Leaf on the Apple Tree* (1955) and *Songs to Eternity* (1959). Leivick's years in Colorado, although noted as having been remarkably productive for a sick man, are typically mentioned in passing as an interlude between the major phases of the writer's active career. The two most recent anthologies of Yiddish-American literature in translation note that while he was in the JCRS, Leivick wrote some of his best poems, including the verse drama *Abelard and Heloise* as well as the fifty-three poems collected in 1940 as the first part of *Poems from the Garden of Eden*. One poem from a cycle of eleven poems on Spinoza, also in the *Garden*, has found a place in the anthologies. However, omitting any specific mention of the "Ballad," Leivick's one extended meditation on life in the sanatorium, leaves the impression that, apart from several shorter lyrics specifically set in the JCRS, the scene of writing from 1932 to 1935 was little more than a coincidental backdrop.[4] Bringing Colorado to the foreground opens a perspective in which it becomes clear that Leivick's years in the Garden of Eden were crucial to what came before and what would follow.

1976, 272), even as he was among those "defining the writer and poet as modern heirs to the prophetic tradition, since they were now the conscience of the Jews and the voices rousing them to righteousness" (273).

4. Harshav and Harshav (1986), 676; see also Chametzky et al. (2001), 282. Leivick's biography has yet to be written. When it is, certain repeated errors of fact will be corrected. Leivick did not spend "four years" but three in Colorado, and at the JCRS Sanatorium, not the "Spivak sanitorium," as the institution was never called (Harshav and Harshav, 676). Similarly, the Chametzky et al. Norton Anthology placed him in "Spivak Sanatorium" from "1932 to 1936" (286). The best overview of Leivick's career remains that of Madison (1968), 348–81.

On the Threshold

In Leivick's sequel to the story of *Abelard and Heloise*, the unfortunate lover Abelard, weakened by the effects of torture, is confined to his cell in a monastery. The most moving of the Spinoza poems lingers over the philosopher's death from pulmonary disease, whether from silicosis developed during his years as a lens grinder, or from tuberculosis: "His sick chest heaves, straining, / racked, racked by fits of coughing" (Spinoza cycle, poem 2, in Chametzky et al. 2001, 285). In fact, Leivick's Colorado works include much more than *Abelard* and the Spinoza sequence. His verse drama *Sodom* replays the destruction of the wicked city with an obvious allusion to the rise of Hitler. *The Sacrifice*, dramatizing Abraham's test on Mount Moriah, is dedicated "To the memory of all who lost their lives innocently as a sacrifice on any altar, whether a group of stones, a hole in a jail, a bed in a hospital, or even the stoop of a house." In this poem Leivick's Isaac asks, "But why should I be the sacrifice? Why did God not ask me if I want to be it?" (Madison 1968, 367).[5] A third play, *The Poet Became Blind*, pays homage to the memory of Morris Rosenfeld. In its climactic scene, Rosenfeld is too sick to attend a celebration in his honor but is honored instead by a chorus of admirers singing his own *lider* at his bedside. The themes of these works—confinement, illness, the bedside, the looming threat of death for an individual or a race, the injustice of an unsought martyrdom—impinge directly on Leivick's life in the JCRS. Or to put it the other way, Leivick projects his life into these dramas, seeing himself as an Abelard, an Isaac, a Rosenfeld, in the comradeship of their suffering, just as he imagines (almost as a powerful hallucination) that Spinoza has rematerialized at the JCRS: "How did he get into this sickroom, / the philosopher

5. In a story one can only hope for his sake is apocryphal, it is recounted the eleven-year-old Leivick "took the part of the sheep in a yeshiva performance of *Isaak's Sacrifice* and was traumatized when the sheep's 'blood' (i.e., beet juice) spilled over his sheep skin" (Madison 1968, 368). In the Spinoza poem cited above, the poet focuses on a "drop of blood" dotting the lip of the apparitional philosopher.

from Amsterdam?" (Chametzky et al. 2001, 285). Leivick will much later recast himself as the stricken Job in the verse drama of 1953, wondering whether the men outside his room urging him on in his lamentations are "really living men" or "feverish imaginings" (Howe and Greenberg 1972, 130).

The first of Leivick's sanatorium lyrics serves as a portal into the *Garden of Eden* collection, comprising work from the years 1932–1936:

> Open up, gate,
> Threshold, you tell ——
> I am coming again
> To an intimate cell.
>
> My body—fire,
> My head—snow;
> And on my shoulders
> A bag of woe.
>
> Farewell, Farewell.
> Hands. Eyes. Bowed.
> A goodbye on the lips
> Flared—burnt out.
>
> From whom did I part?
> Farewell to what past? ——
> Perennial questions
> This time don't ask.
>
> In fire, in flame
> The prairie spreads,
> And snow in the glare
> On mountainous heads.
>
> I bring to your feet
> My bag of woe,
> Land Colorado
> Of fire and snow. (Harshav and Harshav 1986, 737)

In a different translation (by Cynthia Ozick, in Chametzky et al. 2001, 284), the poem is given the title "Sanatorium." This addition specifies the poem's setting but at the cost of prematurely dispelling the uncertainty of the opening lines: what "gate" lies before us, and on what "threshold" do we stand? To be *afn shvel*, on the threshold, is to be in a liminal space between two worlds, an exit and an entry, coming and "coming again."[6] The *shvel* denotes a precarious or marginal position, poised on the brink—a moment when time is suspended, or else momentarily expanded to encompass the present and past. The "intimate cell" that lies on the other side is the best that English can do with Leivick's *tzimerl-tzel*, the hyphenated disjunction of a "cozy little room" and a prison "cell," Colorado and Siberia. In "Again a Neighbor Died" the body of the man in the next bed is carried "over the threshold" to the *tehayre-shtibl*, again a "little" room, but here, in the Yiddish, the room set aside to prepare a corpse for burial (Harshav and Harshav 1986, 738–39). For the dead neighbor, the *shvel* leads both to another room in the sanatorium and to the realm of the dead. A later, post-Holocaust poem begins:

> I was not in Treblinka
> And in Maidanek, not.
> But I stand on their threshold
> Very near the spot.

The poem ends with the lines, "And I stand waiting for my turn, / In Treblinka's fires to burn" (Leivick 1940, 121).

"Open up, gate" is a prelude and a valediction—"Farewell, Farewell"—to a past life, and perhaps to life itself. But as the poem's

6. *Afn Shvel* is, coincidentally, the name of a magazine started in 1941 as an outgrowth of the territorialist movement of the twenties and thirties to promote the idea of a homeland for European Jewry—a people either on the threshold of destruction or of their salvation in some promised land—possibly in Africa or Australia if not in Palestine; it continues today with the mission of preserving Yiddish language and culture (The League for Yiddish, http://www.leagueforyiddish.org / ishi.html).

view expands from the confines of the cell to glance at the prairie to the east and the mountains to the west of the JCRS, what seems to have "burnt out" is suddenly rekindled in the glare of sunlight on the snow, perhaps offering the promise of a new day. Even here, however, the poem leaves open the question of what that day portends for Leivick, death or life? In the past he might have asked, but not "this time." The "flame" of the sun (or is it a prairie fire?) intensifies the fire in his body, as if the fever of the tubercular patient had spread to the very landscape. To the "feet" of these "mountainous heads" he brings (literally, "lays down") his "bag of woe." Will he now be free of his burden? Will the gods of the Rockies be propitiated by this "burnt" offering? To such "perennial questions" the poem can only offer the answer every Yiddish speaker understands: *freg nikht*, "don't ask."

From the Garden of Eden

For *Lider fun Gan-Eydn*, the collection this poem introduces, I prefer the more literal translation *Poems from the Garden of Eden* to *Songs of Heaven* (Harshav and Harshav 1986) or *Songs of Paradise* (Chametzky et al. 2001). Poems written in, or from, Eden—or its latter-day replica, "Land Colorado"—recall a lost origin, a beginning that marks the moment of exile and a destination at the end of a journey. (A spectacular red-rock formation between Denver and Colorado Springs, on the itinerary of every day-trip from the JCRS, is known as "The Garden of the Gods.") The irony of Leivick's title is perhaps implied in the difference between the God of Genesis who walks in the garden and speaks with man in the cool of the evening, and the elemental mountain gods of fire and snow looming over the grounds of the sanatorium. The "cell" that awaits him inevitably recalls Leivick's four years of solitary confinement, followed, in 1912, by a 2,000-mile trek to Siberia, where he was sentenced to life-long exile. It will reappear in the years of the sanatorium poems as the monastic cell of Abelard's captivity. The "snow" on the mountains in "Open up, gate" and the world "snowed in" on the day of his neighbor's death both recall the snow in "On the Roads of Siberia," a poem of 1919 (Harshav and Harshav 1986, 679), as well as the snow "hard and glazed," and the "Snowed-in wolves and bears" in another poem about his escape from Siberia (683). It will recur in the extraordinary "Song of the Yellow Patch" from the forties, in which the poet wonders how, if he were to wear it on the street, the yellow patch of a "Jew in Naziland" would look "On the white ground of a New York snow." There he remembers "building a Mount Sinai of snow" in his childhood, and he imagines that "Somewhere wanders a man / Deeply covered in snow" (745–47). These lines return us to the closing verse of "Somewhere Far Away," his very first published poem, again about the trek to Siberia:

> Deeply covered in snow
> Somewhere wanders a man
> He cannot find a road
> To the land, the forbidden land. (689)

In a later poem, "Yiddish Poets" are like "frazzled cats, dragging / Their kittens around," only "We drag out poems between our teeth / By the neck through the streets of New York" (741). Trudging through Siberia or walking the streets of New York, the itinerary of Leivick's poetry of suffering always takes him on the road, the wandering Jew. On the trek in Siberia he comes to a gate: "I knock, and I freeze: / —— I am frozen, good people, / Open please" (683), but he is not admitted. In 1932 he will be admitted to a cozy little room at the JCRS before resuming his journey. He will have the benefit of a rest cure in a way station, a death house for some, but fortunately for him, a place of healing, in the middle of the road. The sanatorium poem "*Mima'amakim*," echoing Psalm 130, is a cry *de profundis*: "I am calling to you / Fromthedepths [sic]" (743). There is hope. Isaac is spared, Abelard is sprung from his cell by Heloise in disguise, and Leivick recovers his health. Spinoza is at death's door, but having lingered there for "Three hundred years—as though one minute" he will be revived by the touch of the poet: "Holy one, I touch your sleeve. / Wake up, Rise up. Recognize me" (Chametzky et al. 2001, 285).

Spinoza

The poet's "touch" not only enrolls Spinoza in Leivick's untimely community of tuberculars. Its effect accords, if only in fantasy, with the medical view that writing in and for the patient community is therapeutic. Here, poetry even seems to have the capacity to restore the dead to life. In the first poem of the Spinoza sequence, the poet is surprised to find Spinoza sleeping in the next bed—the bed, we may imagine, vacated by the dead "neighbor." The first stirring of Spinoza's recovery will come in the second poem when he can respond to the poet's "Wake up" call, but the sign of his full return to consciousness will only come when he, Spinoza, can "Recognize me," just as earlier in the poem Leivick has recognized Spinoza: "I look at him—there's no uncertainty, / It's he, it's he" (Chametzky et al. 2001, 285). In a later poem Leivick will call the Yiddish poet a *fremde gest*, a "strange" or "alien" guest "on God's earth" (Harshav and Harshav 1986, 741), the sort of unwelcome guest who might have knocked at the gate of a peasant house on the way to Siberia. Here the strange specter of the long-dead philosopher is welcomed as a guest in the poet's little room. What is implied in this mutual recognition? In this imagined transaction across the centuries, the poet's gift of life will be repaid by the philosopher's recognition—his recognition of the poet as a fellow sufferer, but also his recognition of *Leivick*, and of Leivick *as* a life-giving poet. If poetry can will Spinoza back to life, perhaps it can do the same by reflection for Leivick—a moment of hope that counterbalances the gloom of the poem on his neighbor's death: "My pen has no answer for me —— / How could it?" (739). Poets want to be "recognized," as indeed Leivick was at the JCRS, where his own work and example proved an incentive to other patients. At a send-off party on his departure from the JCRS, more than two hundred patients (including my father) gathered to wish him well on his upcoming lecture tour in South America. Recognition confers a kind of immortality on the poet; his fame, it is said, lives after him. In Leivick's case the polarities are reversed. His fame seems to have preceded him by some three hundred years. And if, after three hundred years, Spinoza's is still a name to conjure with, why not Leivick's? Through some alchemy of fire and snow, the works of the sanatorium years fuse into a drama of death and resurrection both chronologically and imaginatively central to Leivick's career.

Like the "Ballad" at the end of the *Poems*, the sequence of eleven Spinoza poems responds in its way to the question never far from the core of Yiddish-American writing: What does it mean to be a Jew in America or, in Leivick's case between 1932 and 1935, what does it mean to be a tubercular Jew among a community of the afflicted, a *fremde gest* in "Land Colorado"? He tells *The Denver Post* that he writes "for a people far away," a people that remembers, as he does, "a heart and mind that was purely Jewish." For Leivick, to be "purely" Jewish can no longer mean to observe *kashruth*, the laws of ritual purity that once bound orthodox Jews together as Jews and marked their separation from the impure ways of the *fremde* in a non-Jewish world. No Zionist, his concern is with "souls," not "soil." Those for whom he writes seem to be not only "far away" from America and even from Jews in America. Presumably, then, he writes for a European or an even more widely diasporic audience, but among these only for Jews who "remember" a purely Jewish heart and mind. To be a Jew *now* can only mean to recover the memory of *what it once was* to be a Jew. But can that memory be revived in any effectual form, or it is to melt away under the Colorado sun like a Mount Sinai made of snow? For this purpose Leivick cannot appeal to the lineage of *kohanim*, rabbis, and religious teachers from whom he is descended, or to the Talmudic education of his childhood—a connection he severed not only by leaving the Yeshiva and turning to radical politics, but by turning away from Hebrew to write in the language of the *volk*. But if Judaism is, in some way, to be purified of the Jewish religion, from where can its "heart and mind" be retrieved? Under the shadow of death, Yiddish alone will not serve: the poet's pen has "no answer." The question becomes particularly urgent to secular immigrant writers poised on the *shvel* between a European past—whether sentimentalized or repudiated—and the allure of an American future promising much, but threatening to dissolve the bonds of a "Jewish" community.

The Spinoza poems implicitly respond to the question by forging an imaginative bond across time between the poet and the seventeenth-century "Jewish" philosopher, both of them suffering from lung disease. It cannot have escaped Leivick's notice that Spinoza was in his mid-forties when he died, just Leivick's age when the poet entered the JCRS. Like the poet, the philosopher abandoned his early religious training, a turn that led eventually to Spinoza's excommunication by the Sephardic community of Amsterdam. We cannot know how much of the philosopher's complex and radical thought on ethics and metaphysics Leivick had absorbed—one does not think of him as a "philosophical" poet. But in Spinoza's reading of scripture, the prophets were not "naturally gifted philosophers," but "simply very pious, even morally superior individuals endowed with vivid imaginations" (Stanford). Spinoza was "considered a hero by secular Jewish intellectuals" (Chametzky et al. 2001, 284n2) for his radical stance, as well as for his never disavowing his Judaism or his belief in the necessary (logical) existence of God, even as he undermined every foundation of orthodox belief.

The first poem of the sequence, "Intellectual Love," opens with the poet apparently citing, or mulling over, two of the philosopher's precepts in the moment before the night nurse arrives to take the book from his hands and turn out the light: "Intellectual love of God —— —— / There is no good, no evil —— ——" (Leivick 1940, 483). Awakened by the poet, in the third poem Spinoza is troubled. Having left hate and resentment behind and found love, has he now been recalled to life only to die again (484–85)? The poet cries out that he hears a voice: "I am the light, / That flows from death into the world"; but "these are the words of bright illusion / That people dare not hear." Leivick's word *van*, which I translate as "illusion" is a loan word from the German *wahn*, which can mean fantasy, fallacy, chimera, hallucination or, as *wahnsinn*, madness. The syntax allows us to wonder whether these are Leivick's words or those of the voice he hears (but people dare not hear), just as the ambiguous *van* can attribute the "words" either to imagination or to madness. The poem ends with a flashback to the snows of Siberia: "I am pursued like a wolf by a hunter; / I sing the song of bright illusion / On white ground in a white bed" (poem 4, 485–86). The title of the poem, "*Nit Geherter*," "The One Who Is not Heard," suggests at once that the word of Spinoza's God is not heard in this world, and that the human singer of those words is not heard by Spinoza's God. Can a "Jewish" religion so purified be anything more (or less) than a "bright illusion?" How brightly can the "light of the world," reflecting both a Christian ethos of love and the "intellectual" spirit of an enlightened Jewish philosopher, shine through the Yiddish poet?

The ninth poem, beginning, "See, how small is my desire" ends in a prayer—Leivick's, or Spinoza's—implying that human desire is boundless and yet, however poignantly imagined, unlikely to be fulfilled:

> To lift up my voice in a prayer:
> —— I call to you, God from the depths, ——
> And God hears my call,
> And lowers himself to your *shvel*.
>
> To move God with my face,
> And then to lay down with him
> Limb to limb, and fall asleep
> With him on the step of your *shvel*.
>
> And in my sleep to see you open
> The door – to come in and lay down
> Between the both of us,
> And to sleep with us on your *shvel*. (Leivick 1940, 489–90, last three stanzas)

The threshold of Leivick's room in the sanatorium would now be the meeting place of the human and the divine—if there were any possibility of Spinoza's transcendent God being moved by a human face and lowering himself in response to human desire. He "hears my call," but does he answer? To be "purely" Jewish in Spinoza's philosophy would be to love a god somehow imbued in the world but divested of all human attributes and reduced, or rather exalted, to the level of an abstract necessity. All the more intense, then, must be the human desire for such a god not only to hear a cry from the depths, but for the god who is otherwise the object of a Spinozan "intellectual love" to lie down next to His tubercular supplicant, "Limb to limb" in an intimate embrace. (It would not be lost on Leivick's Yiddish reader that the word *ober*, or "limb" becomes a penis in the phrase *menlekher ober*, the "male limb.") The prayer conceals a desire for God not only to cross the threshold that separates him from humanity, but to "come in" and lie down to sleep with (and perhaps to impregnate?) Leivick and Spinoza, thus exposing Himself to their illness and incarnating His "intellectual" love in the tubercular body. When you are pursued by a wolf, it is difficult to be consoled by the philosophical principle that "There is no good, no evil." Let God cough his lungs out as a test of that principle.

The final poem in the Spinoza sequence is unlike any of the others: stripped down, disembodied, and reduced to a set of mathematical formulas deployed, as Leivick's title suggests, into four four-line stanzas:

Two Times Two Is Four
The body sheds
Its passionate skin:
What does my pure soul do?
She counts, she counts.

Two times two is —— four.
I times I is —— you.
You times you is —— us.
Death times Death is —— rest.

My head to the east.
My feet to the west:

Go faster, don't stop. ——
Near times near is —— far.

A rustle by the door. —— knock, knock.
It's open. Look in.
Shine in the last look. ——
Death times death is —— to be [or "being"]. (1940, 490–91)

Unencumbered by the body, these dispassionate calculations of the soul precisely describe a "pure" state of being. Here the "intellectual love" presaged in the first poem can finally be imagined as the product "us"—the product of "you" and "I." But "to be" in the end is not to be, or rather to "be" in a place only accessible through death's door. A cool Spinozan logic drives this poem to its rigorous and paradoxical conclusion. The impure residue left behind in this analysis is the corpse laid out for burial in the traditional Jewish manner, "the head to the east" in the direction of Jerusalem.

The Ballad of Denver Sanatorium

Although Spinoza will return in the "Ballad of Denver Sanatorium" (1934), Leivick's longest and concluding poem in the *Poems from the Garden of Eden*, this poem abandons these minimalist metaphysics for a more expansive and passionate narrative that returns to the life of the JCRS (just) on this side of the grave. Its absence from the anthologies is due to its length (112 quatrains), to the difficulty of culling out a piece of its story, and perhaps as well to the poem's indulgence in moments of sentiment by which Leivick captures the schmaltzier tone of sanatorium verse: "A little tear —— you can hardly catch it —— / Boils like an ocean: violent, turbulent" (Leivick 1940, 499).[7] Yet the "Ballad" also contains some of Leivick's finest lines, attuned to the "mystery of suffering" (509) and inspired by his years in "the kingdom of tuberculosis":

7. Subsequent quotations from the "Ballad," indicated by page number in the *Works* of 1940, refer to the translation given in full in the Appendix.

> The song of time is first sung out in holiness
> Here in the kingdom of tuberculosis:
> Through flutes —— the cellular web of lungs ——
> The thinnest seconds are breathed out in full. (502)

Leivick's song in the "Ballad" commemorates the final days of "Nathan Newman," a figure based on an actual patient named Jonathan Newman who breathed out his last second on March 26, 1933, and who was given a pauper's burial two days later in the section of the Golden Hill cemetery reserved for victims of the white plague. Appropriately, in the kingdom of tuberculosis, the poet's song, too, is breathed out through the "flutes" of diseased lungs. Just thirty-four when he died, Jonathan Newman had fruitlessly chased the cure for more than ten years, and from one sanatorium to the next. Although tuberculosis condemned this obscure invalid to an itinerant life and an early death, something magnetic about Jonathan Newman must have drawn Leivick to his subject. Born in Russia in 1899, the son of a rabbi, and a Hebrew teacher by trade, Newman is described in his JCRS medical records as a "brilliant young man," "one of the most intellectual patients the JCRS ever had." As the "Ballad" suggests, Leivick must have been struck, as others were, by Newman's intensity—by the strength of spirit that can be summoned out of the thinnest body, by his "burning dreams" fueled alike by desire and disease (502), and by his ultimate acceptance of death.

Yet for all its particularity of detail about Newman's final days, the "Ballad" is largely fictional in recreating its own "Nathan" Newman out of the actual "Jonathan" Newman who was, in fact, never Leivick's neighbor in the JCRS. Admitted to the JCRS in 1924, Jonathan Newman was discharged in October 1929, nearly three years before Leivick's arrival. By the time the poet met him, Newman had already been to another sanatorium in California. Apparently dissatisfied with his care in California, he returned to Denver and found a bed, his last, across town from the JCRS at the National Jewish Hospital. For dramatic effect, Leivick imagines that his

"Nathan" Newman has been lying "for fifteen years" in "His little room in Denver's hospital" (500). Leivick readily agreed to pay Jonathan Newman a visit when he was told by mutual friends—fellow patients Ben and Bessie Glass—how ardently he was admired by the desperately ill young man. In all likelihood Leivick saw him only a few times before Newman's death and was certainly not present at his deathbed.[8] The poem's account of the simple everyday realities of sanatorium life is based more directly on Leivick's experience as a patient than on Newman's, although the poet came away with a clear impression of Newman's room. The notation of a "small table" beside Newman's bed, "and on it, two little books, / A thermometer, a pitcher, and glass" precisely arranged like the domestic details in a Dutch still life, offers a sketch of the indigent patient's pared down existence (502). "A watch. A Pen": in his simplicity of spirit Leivick's Nathan Newman is of a piece with his, and Leivick's, surroundings (503). Here, far from the opulence of the Alpine sanatorium in *Magic Mountain* or, closer to home, of the elite Cragmor Sanatorium in Colorado Springs, the celebrated poet and his obscure admirer meet.

To a large extent, "Nathan Newman" supplies Leivick with a blank canvas that the poet can fill in with details of his own ongoing, grandly mythic autobiography. There is no evidence that Leivick and the real Jonathan Newman ever had (or did not have) a conversation about the latter's early years in Russia. In the "Ballad," the child

8. Bessie Glass remembered being summoned into Leivick's room to hear the excited poet read her and her husband Ben a draft of the "Ballad" he had just then finished. As the poem notes, Newman did have a "faithful sister" (503) in the Bronx who would eventually send the money for Jonathan's headstone. There is no evidence outside the poem of "Nathan" Newman's other correspondent, she who is said to be a "sister and something more" (503). The poet, his memory evidently hazier than his imagination, wanted to know if he had gotten things right. Bessie Glass recalled having to correct him on the color of Newman's hair (author's interview with Bessie Glass, Denver, Colorado, August 1988).

"Nathan" Newman is said to have been so "Captivated" by the sight of a prison apparently near his home in the shtetl that he

would not
Stray far from the black prison door to walk
With the exiles even for a block
On their march to the eternal Siberia.

He was too young for prison chains,
But not too young to catch this deadly thing,
To wander from one hospital to the next,
Until he winds up here at Spivak House. (501)

Backdating Newman's illness to his childhood, the passage elides political exile and tubercular wandering, Siberia and the sanatorium. Then too young for prison chains, Nathan Newman is now "Shackled to his bed" (502), but he is nonetheless "Marching in chains" toward a new world at the head of a lineage of "martyrs and warriors" (501). Leivick says, "The dying Newman / Captivated me, chained utterly / To his room" (506). Newman's chains will return in a very different context, as we will see, but here they serve to bind the poet and his subject in their mutual captivation. A commemorative postcard reissued after Leivick's death in 1962 shows the young revolutionary in chains after his capture by the Czarist police (figure 6).

The prisoner stands erect, staring into the distance as if absorbed in a vision beyond his immediate plight, his long coat open so as to display his leg shackles and the chain locking them to his belt. Somewhere in the imaginary past of the "Ballad," the child Newman—who still bears the "shame / Of oppression" on his "thin shoulders" (501)—may be imagined to have caught a glimpse of the twenty-four-year-old Leivick among those prisoners being marched out of a Russian prison and off to their Siberian exile.

Entering Newman's room shortly before the invalid's death takes the poet over the final *shvel* to be crossed in the *Poems from the Garden of Eden*:

6. Leivick in chains. The young revolutionary was destined for a Czarist prison in 1906. Image from a commemorative French postcard, "H. Leivick (Poèt), 1888 – décembre – 1962," and issued by the "Coultoure Congresse," Paris. As testimony to Leivick's international fame, a French translation of his poetry would appear in 1968 with an introduction by Marc Chagall.

> As soon as I cross the threshold, he
> Feels it right away and says hello,
> And smiles: "Today I am a hero,
> I've pushed the final hour back a step." (507)

In Leivick's "song of time," this small and temporary victory over the final hour reflects the opening question of the "Ballad": "These days how can you weave what legends say / Just from the death of somebody unknown?" How does Newman qualify as a fit subject for a genre already overpopulated by saints and Arthurian knights? The answer is that Newman "kept the lineage / Of martyrs, warriors —— dream figures" in his heart as "The bright image of an heroic age" (501). In the theology of Leivick's tubercular kingdom, Nathan Newman is no "Jesus dying" on the cross or "Moses on the *shvel* of Canaan" (499); but now on the brink of death he inherits the suffering of the one and the unfulfilled hopes of the other. At the same time, the biblical stories of Jesus and Moses are implicitly recast as "what legends say," episodes in the history of a secular and ecumenical vision encompassing all narrower dogmas. Beginning a Yiddish poem, as the "Ballad" begins, with the line "It isn't Jesus dying, nailed to the cross" (499) must be read as an intentional provocation on Leivick's part—a gesture that simultaneously evokes and repudiates the Christian redeemer. In this lineage of non-denominational martyrs and warriors, the Jew Newman combines the deepest human impulses of Christianity and Judaism forged in the crucible of his suffering. In his room we stand before the image of "Life's holiness" (499) reflected in the body and the blood: "His body —— the lightest, the most refined" (501) almost to a transparency, and the "rush of blood" that flows "from his cracked throat / Onto the white pillow" (504).

The centerpiece of the "Ballad," Leivick's visit to the young man's room is imagined in retrospect as an event that happened yesterday and is now recalled by Newman in a feverish, phantasmal dream (505–06). We know that Newman thrashes from side to side, "consumed in desire, in burning dreams" (502). On this day he dreams of a "light in the wall" that dances and "springs into flame," a "man's hand —— maybe his neighbor's hand," a hand that seems somehow to have "crawled through the wall," a hand that is even now reaching toward his bed: the hand, he begins to realize, of "the Yiddish poet." This strange apparition "hurls himself around as in a cell" and "carries the form of a song within" that he seeks to perfect on a "bloody threshold." Only the disembodied "hand" represents the Yiddish poet, who, as sheer movement, light, dance, and flame, seems to be dissolved into a charge of restless energy seeking to perfect the very "song" that will become the "Ballad." Newman's dream has absorbed Leivick into the "lineage" of "dream figures" that the mortally ill young man "keeps hidden in his heart": the "bright image of an heroic age, / The vision of a clear, eternal truth" (501). The dreamer now remembers that the "neighbor" who came to visit the day before "had talked of Heine's and Spinoza's pain / And death," and he wonders whether this "hand" in his dream has "now come to braid / All their deaths in a single, wondrous chain" (505).

The chained prisoner marching to Siberia and the patient chained to his bed—both under a death sentence—are now woven into a new lineage of heroic tubercular Jews martyred by the same disease. Spinoza reappears as a link in this chain, noted for his belief that death "ought / To be itself a streaming forth, / The loving radiance of the divine thought." Heinrich Heine "lay for eight years" and "bravely fought not to shut his eyes" (505). Heine was in fact bedridden for the eight years before his death, but from some mysterious paralysis and not from tuberculosis; and, although born to a secular Jewish family, he early on converted to Christianity and even adopted "Christian" as his middle name. But for Leivick, both the apostate Jewish poet and the heretical Jewish philosopher were "Jewish" enough. Newman hopes that the serene "Spinoza will not be mad at me / For opening my heart to anger's lure" (511). But it is Heine's passion for life that supplies what Spinoza's serenely thoughtful preparation for death lacks. These opposed practices in the art of dying define the difference between the philosopher and the "romantic" poet (505). Leivick's own practice of the art of poetry in the "Ballad" clearly owes more to Heine than to Spinoza, however much the latter is to be admired. Newman "smiles" at the "impertinence" of comparing oneself to "The godlike Spinoza / And to Heine the romantic poet" (505); but as their heir in suffering, Newman combines the two, first in his rage and then his final "yes" to death.

A Spiritual Petrel

In the ballad, the "third to Heine and Spinoza" (505) in Leivick's trinity of godlike predecessors is the Yiddish poet Dovid Edelshtat (usually Anglicized as "David Edelstadt"). Russian born, Edelshtat emigrated from Russia at fifteen, in 1882, going first to Cincinnati and thereafter to New York. A button-hole maker by trade and an anarchist and labor organizer by political conviction, Edelshtat contracted tuberculosis and moved from New York to Denver in 1891.

He died there a year later, in October 1892, at the age of twenty-six. Like Jonathan Newman's life, Edelshtat's was one of brilliant promise cut tragically short. Edelshtat lived and died in Denver as a private boarder: the founding of the JCRS was still in the future. But his spirit was still very much alive in the sanatorium long after, just as his remains lay nearby. As Leivick's Nathan Newman knows, Edelshtat lies "in Denver" (505), in the Jewish cemetery just up Colfax Avenue from the JCRS. His gravestone stands in the special section reserved for tuberculosis victims, near that of the real Jonathan Newman, who would be buried there forty-one years later. In the brief time granted him in New York before he fell ill, Edelshtat quickly became a rock star in the circle of journalists, agitators, and literary figures associated with the Jewish anarchist organization, "The Pioneers of Liberty." Fellow Pioneer Emma Goldman wrote that "Among the frequenters [at our gatherings] were some very able young men whose names were well known in the New York ghetto; among others, David Edelstadt, a fine idealistic nature, a spiritual petrel whose songs of revolt were beloved by every Yiddish-speaking radical" (1931, 55). Edelshtat served the movement as a propagandist and fundraiser. He also edited the Yiddish newspaper *Freie Arbeiter Stimme* (the Free Voice of Labor). But as Goldman notes, the young poet was beloved above all for his "songs of revolt."[9]

These songs are collected in Edelshtat's *Writings*, published posthumously in 1909, a volume obsessed with the two themes inextricably bound up in the poet's brief life: the struggle for revolution, and the struggle against death. "The whole world / Is but a long chain / of black and white links / Called life and death," he writes in "Immortality": the only hope is "a living tree" might spring from the "clay of dead fighters" (203). "My Last Hope" is that in the "minute before

9. Edelshtat singing societies were established in New York during his lifetime, and in a number of other cities thereafter (see Foner 1975, 318–19; Kramer 1989, 59–62). There is no full biography of Edelshtat in English. A biography of Edelshtat was published in Yiddish by the Marxist critic Kalman Marmor (New York, 1942). Details of his life are to be found in Madison (1968, 139–40).

my death" the "people will break their chains" (139–140). "My Last Wish" (163) is to die on the battlefield and not of tuberculosis: "I do not fear death —— I am frightened by the thought / of dying in a sick-bed" (163). But then, "From My Diary": "How stupid to fight against death: / Life is a thousand times worse" (164). Haunted as much by the specter of tuberculosis as by the specter of revolution, Edelshtat is visited by "Frightful Guests," the ghosts of those who have been murdered for their love of freedom; when they come to him at night he breaks out in "a cold sweat" (110). In "To King Death" he writes:

I am still young, I want to try
Myself in battle
To attack inhumanity and tyranny
With renewed strength. (166)

His strength was not to be renewed. In the poem "1891," written when he seemed destined not to live until 1892, Edelshtat notes that "the old year has died," but a "new year is born" for others to continue the struggle. Two poems in the collection reflect on his poetry. At the beginning, he speaks "To My Pen," as his beloved, his only friend: "I breathe free in your writing" (4). Later he writes "To the Muse":

Muse! You're knocking at the door again
Of my poor, suffering heart;
My child, I have no place for you ——
My heart is full of tears and pain.

Just look, I am sick and tired,
How can I now sing songs?
And how can my song of sorrow
Help my poor sisters and brothers?
[. . . .]
To you, who know of golden hours,
Of sweet and heavenly charm, ——
And me, with my chains and wounds,
Leave me alone for a while! (204–05)

Linked to this dead poet by the chains of suffering, Leivick imagines that his Nathan Newman, still dreaming, receives "a greeting, intimate and / Warm, from the face of Dovid Edelshtat."

The hand of the "Yiddish poet" returns, and "now on the walls of the room" it "inscribes a poem." The writing that appears on the wall is, in fact, the first stanza of Edelshtat's most famous revolutionary song, "My Testament" (quoted in Leivick 1940, 506):

> Oh, my good friends, when I shall die,
> Carry the red flag to my grave,
> The red flag with the colors bright,
> Spattered with the blood of working men.

Newman begins to sing the song. He gets as far as the second line—which, as he sings it, is changed to "Carry the red flag to my grave too"—when suddenly the red flag of tubercular death gurgles up in his throat, "And Newman chokes it back, too weak to sing" (506). Thus begins Newman's "last wandering" (506), and the poem will linger over his death for another fifty-one stanzas, as Leivick is "dissolved into mystery of suffering, / of seeing the exhalation of the lung / Through the open window into the sun" (509). With Newman too weak to sing, the poet will finish the song for him. At this moment, the layering of voices gives the "Ballad" its fullest resonance as the strange "neighbor"—or is it just the neighbor's "hand"—appears to Newman in his dream. The ghostly visitor, as we have seen, "hurls himself around" carrying within him the "form of a song" that he is struggling to finish. "Maybe" it's the hand of "the Yiddish poet?" (505). But which Yiddish poet: Leivick? Edelshtat? For the latter's face will then appear, and "the hand / Again"—again, whose hand?—will inscribe the first verse of Edelshtat's "Testament" on the dreamer's wall (506). In Leivick's Yiddish, the word I have rendered neutrally as "the *form* of a song" is *gilgl*. The word can mean "formation," "metamorphosis," or "version"; in Jewish lore the *gilgl* is also the being "into which the soul of a dead person may pass to continue life and atone for sins committed in the previous incarnation" (Weinreich 1968, s.v. *gilgl*). Edelshtat's "Testament" is his will, the document that enjoins the responsibility of carrying on the fight upon his heirs in the struggle. But the song, too, is part of the inheritance, bequeathed to successive generations of singers who will keep the spirit of the poet alive as well as that of his cause. Nathan Newman in turn leaves his book and his glass to Leivick (Leivick 1940, 508). The glass recalls the memory of Spinoza, who contracted his disease grinding lenses. We are not told the contents of the book, just that it lay on Newman's table near his bed. We are permitted to imagine that it's a copy of Edelshtat's poems, a volume Leivick had in his possession at the JCRS. In the "Ballad" Newman gives voice to the poem written on the wall; the poem is re-inscribed in the "Ballad" by Leivick's hand, whence it is passed on to be sung by those still on life's side of the threshold.

That Newman is no Jesus and no Moses severs him from the roots of both religions. Instead, by his death he is forged into a "single wondrous chain" (Leivick 1940, 505) of saintly predecessors—Spinoza, Heine, and Edelshtat—three secular Jewish martyrs who in different ways exemplify the holiness of life by the heroism of their early departure from it. You can "weave what legends say / Just from the death of somebody unknown" (499) when that somebody reincarnates the soul of the bodies that have gone before. The scene of writing, *on* the wall and *of* the poem, is the tuberculosis sanatorium. For whom is the writing on the wall? Now in his turn at the head of this tubercular lineage, must the poet share their fate? In 1934 Leivick could not know for sure. Is the "Ballad" to be Leivick's own testament, now entrusted to the reader? In the end Nathan Newman, the poet's instructor in the *ars moriendi*, can say "yes" to death (502). The example of Newman's transcendent suffering imposes the burden of writing and eases the burden of mortality.

4

Shtern and *The White House*

Forty Years in Retrospect

Sholem Shtern, born in a shtetl near Lublin, immigrated to Canada in 1927 at the age of twenty. Rundown and suspected of developing tuberculosis, he cured for nearly two years at the Mount Sinai Sanatorium in the Laurentian Mountains in southern Quebec. In 1928 he lived out one of the stock fantasies of lunger lit, courting and then marrying his nurse Sonia, a fellow immigrant (figure 7).

Shtern published steadily during his subsequent working career as a teacher and then principal of a Jewish school in Montreal. He was "a prolific journalist in the Yiddish press, contributing regularly to the Toronto *Vochenblatt* and other publications" (Bibiothêque et Archives, see fn 1) in and outside of Canada. His poems were featured in Yiddish newspapers throughout the world. He produced three books of poetry between 1929 and 1945, followed by three novels in verse and a final collection of essays and memoirs published after he retired from the school in 1959. His first collection of poems, *Noentkayt* (Nearness), appeared in 1929, just after his stay at Mount Sinai, and contains work written while a patient there. *Dos Vayse Hoyz* (The White House), his Yiddish verse novel set in the sanatorium, appeared almost forty years later in 1967, published by YKUF, the marxist Yiddish Cultural Union. *The White House* was subsequently translated into Hebrew (1972), English (1974), and French (1977).[1] Shtern died in 1990.

1. The English version, translated by Max Rosenfeld and published in 1974 under the title *The White House: A Novel in Verse*—considered to be the finest of

7. A pastoral idyll: the poet Sholem Shtern in repose with Sonia—his nurse, his muse, and his fiancée, in the greenwood near Mount Sinai Sanatorium. Photo courtesy of David and Elspeth Shtern.

Why, after four decades, should Shtern have chosen to revisit his years in the sanatorium? *Dos Vayse Hoyz*, the best known of Shtern's works, was the only one of his verse novels to be translated into Hebrew, but all three (except for the second volume of *In Kanade*) were translated into French and English as well. These novels, along with his earlier poetry and newspaper articles, enhanced Shtern's reputation as one of Canada's foremost Yiddish authors.[2] But if he

the translations of his novels into either English or French (Margolis 2007, 99)—is used in this chapter, but with the original Yiddish in view. The main body of Shtern material is archived in the Library and Archives (Bibiothêque et Archives), Canada, located in Ottawa. An overview of their Shtern holdings, including a list of the author's publications and a "Biographical Sketch" (quoted above) is available at http://www.collectionscanada.gc.ca/literaryarchives/027011-200.123-e.html.

2. When he arrived in 1927 Shtern entered into the "heart of the Yiddish cultural movement in Montreal at a moment when it was reaching its golden age. In the course of that decade and the following, the number of Yiddish language institutions reached its apogee" due to the wave of immigration from Eastern Europe. "Because his brother Yaakov Zipper arrived several years before him and was

was to secure a wider audience for his books it was crucial for him that they also be made available in Canada's two official languages. Some who wished to preserve Yiddish were concerned to safeguard it from contamination by the new languages immigrants needed to master in order to succeed in the new world. Neither Yehoash nor Leivick was particularly concerned to see his work translated into other languages. Yehoash's dictionary was intended to fortify Yiddish from within by providing a guide to the Hebraic component of the vocabulary in which uneducated speakers were often deficient. His Yiddish *Hiawatha* brought Longfellow to the Jews, not the Jews to Longfellow. Shtern, however, "campaigned vigorously in Montreal and elsewhere in North America to include Yiddish writing in the life of his community, and by so doing to promote a certain ideal of social justice" in line with his commitment to radical politics (Anctil 2009, 63; my translation). The appearance of his work in English and French, a project in which he took a keen interest, would stake a claim for Yiddish in the larger sphere of Canadian literature—a goal one critic calls Shtern's "Canadianization of Yiddish Canadian writing" (81; my translation). The same impulse can be felt in *The White House* insofar as the novel locates the insular world of the sanatorium and its distinctively Jewish concerns within the broader landscape of the Laurentian mountains and its people. The English translation of the novel in 1974 was underwritten by a grant to promote multiculturalism for which Shtern had applied to the Canadian government.

Bridging the Gap

Shtern's pioneering effort to "make his writing accessible to a non-Yiddish readership" as well as to broaden the scope of Yiddish writing to include encounters with the Québécois is documented in Rebecca

---

teaching in a well-known Yiddish school, the Peretz School in Montreal," Shtern immediately gained entrance into the Yiddish literary and artistic circles of the city. A contemporary survey found 429 Yiddish writers in Canada (Anctil 2009, 72; my translation).

Margolis's "Sholem Shtern: Bridging the Gaps" (2007, 98). Her subtitle points to other "gaps" the writer attempts to bridge, starting with the gap of time spent in the sanatorium between his arrival in Canada and his settlement in Montreal. Accounting for Shtern's success in moving quickly to the center of Canada's Yiddish literary circle, Pierre Anctil argues that because Shtern (the son of a Polish *shochet* and scholar) combined a traditional religious background with a commitment to radical politics, he was able to straddle the fault line "that cut through the Canadian Yiddish milieu" (2009, 72; my translation). On whichever side of "la ligne de fracture" between Moses and Marx they stood in those years, however, Canadian Yiddish writers faced another linguistic and cultural gap separating them from both the "economically dominant English-Protestant minority and the disenfranchised French-Canadian majority" (Margolis 2007, 98) with whom Shtern had hoped to form a bond of solidarity through his writing. In both these cultural relations, intramural and extramural, Shtern played a shifting, amphibious role over a writing career of more than sixty years. Passionate about Yiddish, sometimes unabashedly nostalgic and sentimental about his early life in Poland, he understood that between him and the world of his fathers lay a truly unbridgeable gap. An outspoken radical in his earlier journalism, Shtern, like many others after World War II, gradually became disillusioned with the kind of hardline Party politics to which in the end he was never fully committed (Margolis 2007, 99), but he never abandoned his social activism.[3]

The greatest gap in the timeline of Shtern's writing lies between his descent from the Mount Sinai Sanatorium and the publication of *The White House* forty years later. The delay seems fitting insofar as *The White House* appeared as the second in a trilogy of

3. In an email (8/27/13) David Shtern notes that it was his uncle Yaakov Zipper, brother of the poet, who in his *Journals* (85) first noted Sholem's reservations about the movement. In his literary memoir (*Writers I Have Known* [in English]), the poet denounces Stalin and argues that Jews should never subjugate their identity to serve an ideology.

semi-autobiographical Yiddish novels in verse published between 1960 and 1975.[4] In this context it occupies one phase of Shtern's final project: the writer turns sixty, looks backward, and takes stock. Its importance for Shtern can be gauged by the novel's attention to a brief two-year period in the author's life in the midst of a sequence that otherwise spans the generations of immigrant experience in Canada. But unlike Yehoash and Leivick—whose sanatorium writing emerges from and captures the immediacy of their experience—Shtern has no choice but to reimagine Mount Sinai from a distance, its image refracted through everything that had happened in the intervening decades: the question of identity for a hybridized Yiddish-Canadian writer, the writer's commitment to and ultimate disillusion with the Movement, and above all the impact of the destruction of European Jewry in the Holocaust. In 1927 the sanatorium, with its population of recent immigrants, fostered and to an extent replicated an eastern European community in miniature. In 1949 Shtern visited Poland and knew that he "could not write about the great, wonderful past when everything was lying in ruins": "I sensed," as he later reflected on the first novel in his trilogy, *In Kanade*, "that I had to reorient myself elsewhere" (Shtern 1982, 204–05). By 1967, both the institution of the tuberculosis sanatorium and, at Mount Sinai, the little world of transplanted Yiddish culture it preserved had also disappeared. After such a seismic convulsion, picking through the ruins for the pieces of a novel necessarily yields a supplementary account—one that, in Derrida's words, "adds only to replace," an account that offers itself as "the fullest measure of presence" but also as "the mark

4. The first, *In Kanade* (2 vols.) (Montréal: Sholem Shtern Bukh-komitet, 1960–1963), follows a young immigrant's adjustment to Canada. The third, *Di Mishpokhe in Kanade un Dos Hoyzgesind fun Profesor Sidni Goldstin: Tsvey noveln* (The Family in Canada and the Household of Professor Sidney Goldstein: Two Novellas) (Montréal: S. Shtern, 1975), takes up a broader range of themes in the immigrant experience as they play out over several generations: nostalgia for the old world, acculturation in the new, radical politics, and intermarriage.

of an absence" (1976, 144). Recovering Mount Sinai after forty years is an archeological task akin to that faced in 1924 by Thomas Mann in attempting to conjure up the "magic" of his mountain just before Hans Castorp descends from its heights into the maelstrom of the First World War. Shtern's advantage in this task, of course, is that he has the example of *The Magic Mountain* before him.

Intimacy

Shtern's first collection of poems, a slim volume entitled *Noentkayt* (Nearness, or Intimacy) and published in 1929 just after Shtern left the sanatorium, is dedicated "To Sonia" Elbaum, a fellow immigrant and the nurse who was to become Shtern's wife. The first section, "Joy," contains love poems addressed to Sonia amid paeans to the sun, the snow, and the mountains. The sanatorium setting provides the background, but not the focus of the poetry. The second section, "My Mother's Shabbos," looks back to the world of Shtern's childhood. Can it be pertinent to ask why Shtern chooses *not* to write more explicitly about life in the institution in which he had spent the better part of the preceding two years? Why does he choose to recall the experience as a romantic interlude (as it was, evidently) and an occasion for warm reminiscence, and thus to elide or defer the very theme that will powerfully emerge only later? The question need not arise except as it is prompted by the two concluding poems in the collection: "The Picture" and "Valediction," both ending at the close of day and both written in a very different key from what comes before:

The Picture
Hewn from stone
I made alone
In morning bright
A picture – a splendid one
With eyes – two
That look somewhere far off . . .
With rough eyes
Sorrowful looking –

I felt
I was choking . . .
A tear falling

Sizzled on the grey stone –
One, two!
A turn this way, and that,
A kick with my foot
In the deep set eyes
Crack! Crack! Crack
Shattered into tiny pieces —— —— ——
The eyes still yearn, ——
I look for little stones
By every laughing bank
Every evening. (Shtern 1929, 41–42)

Valediction
In an autumn evening
The sun brightened
And parted from me:
A sunbeam danced
On my typewriter
And said something to me
Like a lover to his love –
And before I could lift my head
The sun set sickly-red
And a desire to wait
Seeped into me. (43)

The "Valediction" ("*Gezegnt*") ends the volume, appropriately, with a sunset. But rather than basking in the afterglow of a task completed, the poem bespeaks a failure to grasp "something." The collection had been dedicated by Shtern to Sonia: a lover to his love. Now the sunbeam speaks to *him* like a departing lover in a final moment of *noentkayt*. Is this a valediction to love or to love poetry?

The sunbeam dances on his typewriter, but whatever flicker of illumination this solar muse promises to offer disappears in the instant, leaving the poet with nothing to make his own fingers dance on the keys—only with words unheard and a "desire to wait." An unfulfilled desire to wait, for what? For the "something" left unsaid to be grasped and put on paper? The final lines hint at what these poems given to love, nostalgia, and the beauties of nature cannot acknowledge about a scene of writing (or typing) from which tuberculosis has been erased: the sun goes down, or is extinguished ("*oysgegangen*") literally in a "sickly," or even stronger, a "diseased redness" ("*krenklekh-roitkeyt*").

"The Picture" ("*Dos Bild*"), coming just before the end, is far more jarring. In enigmatic and ominous language it imagines the creation of a "splendid picture," a figure of stone hewn in the morning, its destruction, punctuated by the sound of the object being kicked to pieces ("*Trakh, trakh, trakh*!" in the Yiddish), and finally, every evening, a search for the fragments along every "laughing" stream or river bank. The poem bristles with violent emotion and unexpressed motives: What do the figure's eyes behold "far off," and what does the poet see in them that provokes his scalding tears, his iconoclastic fury, and, finally, his fruitless yearning—seemingly mocked by cruel laughter—to find all the pieces? And is the desire in the poet/sculptor's eyes or in those of the image (the Yiddish grammar is ambiguous on this point)? Perhaps in both if this "picture" is, or was to be, a self-portrait. And why should the speaker feel himself "choking"? Like the "Valediction" with its blood-red sunset, this poem turns on a tubercular symptom. The poet is not choking back tears, as the English idiom might have it. The emphatic word "*dershtikt*" implies rather that he is choking to death: the word "*trakh*," repeated three times, sounds as much like a hacking cough as it does a foot kicking stone. Taken together, these two final poems carry the force of a retraction—of an impulse born of rage and regret to destroy the splendid picture one has made in a bright morning, but one coupled with a desire to search among the ruins for the broken pieces. For what, and when? One can only turn the desire to write of love rather than death into a "desire to wait" for "something" else.

It Grows Light

The titles of Shtern's next two collections of poetry, published after a hiatus of more than a decade, signal a return to the inspiration of a bright morning: *It Grows Light* (*Es Likhtikt*) in 1941, and *Morning* (*Inderfri*) in 1945. The crucial difference lies in the dates: in 1945, it is the morning after the Holocaust. *Es Likhtikt*, the earlier collection, returns explicitly to Mount Sinai with a sequence of twenty-two poems subtitled "White Grief: In the Sanatorium." Part of this sequence, "The First Snow" (1941, 39) reprises the "The Picture" by imagining that the poet now "goes into the woods, among the stones / And writes in his notebook," thus: "Light snow everywhere / Blessed is the day / The road, and the stones around." The stones on this white, light surface mark the road he will take; they are recollected in his notebook as the bits of material out of which he will fashion a new image of the sanatorium. The sequence has a narrative frame beginning with the arrival at Mount Sinai of a frail young man (appropriately) named Moyshe. It ends with the exuberant poem, "I Am Now Healthy," marking Moyshe's (or Shtern's) recovery: "I feel the joy of life / Born again in me" (60). But along the way—and perhaps because the poet has himself survived the confrontation—these poems now for the first time confront the grey stone face of death. We are back "In the Land of the Dead," where "A crow croaks on a stone" and where snow falls on the roofs and on the muddy roads (37). To his fellow patients of the decade before, the poet says, "I see you still: / Blood flecks on white cloth, / White flame in your limbs" (59). In the poem "After a Blizzard" the lungers in their daybeds "look out over the white wasteland [*vayser-vistkeyt*] and are silent." One man cries out bitterly against his fate; the others feel his pain, and it seems to them that "from the white stillness / death approaches" (40). And in "The Last Room," a patient has died and will soon be "carried out in white sheets" (47). White sheets, a white wasteland of snow, the white cloth, a white stillness. White, the color of death, foreshadows *The White House*, the verse novel for which the sequence of sanatorium poems in the 1941 collection can be seen as a kind of notebook sketch.

It Grows Dark

Inderfri, the later collection, opens with a prayer, "Open Up": "Oh God, open the gate / Of righteousness for me: / The world lies in ruin" (1945, 5). Shtern's word for the world's destruction, *khorbn*—literally, a "sacrifice," a burnt offering in the time of the Temple—is what Yiddish (and Hebrew) speakers call the Holocaust. This is a "morning" like none other. In 1945 a new day dawns, the day after the annihilation of European Jewry. Can something be made of nothing? Shtern's response in this collection is at once more emphatically religious and more overtly political than anything found in his earlier volumes. The intimacies of *Noentkayt* no longer appear; and while the sanatorium poems of *Es Likhtikt* mourn the death of individuals before arriving at the exuberant final poem ("I Am Cured!"), *Inderfri* must confront the death of millions whose lives will not be restored by bed rest and mountain air. "A Prayer" beseeches God "to lift us up again / Raise up your people from the bloody dust." It imagines a time, if the prayer should be answered, when cities and towns will be restored, when warm rooms will once again shelter "honest and ardent Jews, and when Jewish farmers will cultivate their fields in peace" (112). "After the Battle," in contrast, strikes the militant note of Shtern's political journalism. The field is once again "soaked in blood." But the "red warriors," humble in victory, now put away their weapons in favor of the hammer and sickle, tools for building the new world order. In the end, others join them in singing the "song of joy, labor's song" (106).

Rooted in the same bloody soil, these two poems conjure up very different visions of a post-war world. Will the God of Israel restore the Jews' cities and towns, with scholars once more comfortable in *Yiddishe shtiblekh* while Jewish farmers plant their fields, or will the work of reconstruction be accomplished by wielders of the hammer and sickle in the field of revolutionary politics? Can the same poet have written both "A Prayer" and "After the Battle"? The conflict between these two visions will emerge as a central theme of *The White House*. For the moment they converge in the remarkable poem, "Rabbi Akiva Teaches Torah" (Shtern 1945, 233–34):

> Old Rabbi Akiva
> Studies Torah day and night.
> He pours his ardent spirit into the
> Warlike beating hearts
> Of his eager young students.
> He secretly teaches the forbidden Torah.

The occupying Romans have forbidden Torah study—as well they might in the case of (Shtern's) Akiva, whose teaching fans the flames of armed rebellion. Neither anger alone nor piety will "defeat murderous pagan Rome." Forsaking the study hall for the road, the ancient sage dons *tallit* and *tefillin* and walks from town to town, inflaming the hearts of the people and inspiring bar-Kokhba himself: Akiva teaches the rebel leader that "The time of the foretold Messiah has come." The final three lines break the historical frame in order to address the reader directly: "Readers in Israel arise, / Kill the enemy on the high mountains, / In the deep, grassy valleys." Speaking for, and through, the venerable scholar implicates the poet in a complex and finally ironic gesture. On the authority of Akiva, one of the greatest *tanna'im* (Rabbinic sages) of the first century CE, to learn Torah is to be imbued with a spirit of resistance to tyranny. In light of this revisionary history of Judaism, there need be no conflict of belief between Moses and Marx. Akiva preaches revolution in *tallit* and *tefillin*. Akiva's Torah teaches that rather than suffering patiently in hope of the Messiah, we should recognize him when he walks among us embodied in a charismatic military leader like bar-Kokhba—whose sword, as a matter of fact or legend, Rabbi Akiva is said to have carried. But the latter-day Israelites to whom Akiva/Shtern appeals at the end will know more than the poem can acknowledge: that bar-Kokhba's revolt, like that of the resistance fighters in the Warsaw Ghetto, was brutally crushed in the end, and

Akiva himself martyred by the Romans. The Israelites' survival as a people after the proto-Holocaust of the Roman occupation and the destruction the Second Temple in 70 CE was largely the work of Akiva's pen—he is honored as one of the principal codifiers of the Mishnah—and not of bar-Kokhba's sword. But this irony, too, can take another turn. If writing, not fighting, could preserve the identity of a people scattered to the winds after their homeland was ravaged and many thousands slaughtered, was it not now the responsibility of the Jewish writer to take on the same burden after the Holocaust?

The rifts exposed in the Akiva poem—between piety and revolutionary politics, and again between both and a neo-georgic vision of Jewish farmers plowing their fields—will be deepened and bridged in *The White House*. The Mount Sinai Sanatorium houses a community of displaced Jews isolated from but implicated in their new Canadian homeland. The very fact that they form a community—however temporary and precarious, and despite their sharp differences in matters of religion, politics, and literature—argues implicitly for the idea of a Jewish people. For the writer, the mountain sanatorium affords a privileged site removed from the immediacy of historical events and enjoying its own distant vantage over what Thomas Mann calls the "flatland" below. In this respect it takes on the contours of a Utopian seclusion or a Platonic symposium—a theater of ideas. However, like such other literary preserves as the hills above Florence where Boccaccio's storytellers take refuge from the plague, or Mann's Berghof Sanatorium on the verge of the Great War, the Mount Sinai Sanatorium is a community forged in the face of death, one in which stories are tied to survival and ideas are heightened by the fever of their proponents.

The White House

Subtitled "A Novel in Verse," *The White House* may be described more accurately as a partly autobiographical collection of poems expanding on the sanatorium theme of *Es Likhtikt*, and strung along the same narrative line—albeit a longer one—as the love story in *Noentkayt*. The dedication is once again "To Sonia" (1974, 9).

Shtern's protagonist, the budding poet Velvl Greenblatt—a "green" protagonist reminiscent of Mann's Hans Castorp in his youth and naiveté—falls in love with his nurse Miss Alman. Their courtship is hindered by the superintendent Miss Glynn, a martinet who (though herself secretly in love with a doctor) opposes any personal relations between her staff and the patients. Happily, in the end Velvl is restored to health. He marries his Miss Alman, and the newlyweds return to the city whence they both came to Mount Sinai. The central Mount Sinai narrative is thus framed by "the city," a tangle of poles and wires and the subject of one of Velvl's poems, written in a jerky telegraphic style to catch the staccato rhythm of the urban street:

> A stray dog runs to catch a bone.
> An auto squeals:
> the quivering form is crushed
> [. . . .]
> A workman's [sic] slips.
> Body falls, is shattered.
> Head is split.
> City! Curse the city! (123)

Safe in the Laurentians from squealing autos and shattered bodies, Velvl watches as the painter Gorin depicts a scene very much in contrast to Velvl's image of the city as a hubbub of "picket signs and hunger marches":

> fruitful fields,
> brilliant skies that hover
> over sturdy stalks weighted down with corn.
> Sweet-smelling summer in the orchards.
> Sunlight. Juice of ripe black cherries. (33)

For the poet the sanatorium offers a pastoral interlude with a Canadian rather than an Arcadian setting. Velvl "Greenleaf" writes home: "I marvel at this miracle of renewal. / Lilacs in the gardens gleam like jewels" (55).

Although the other patients of Velvl's acquaintance are provided with brief backstories, none emerges as a fully developed character. Rather, each is given a sharply drawn role to play in the fractious Jewish political and artistic milieu of Shtern's formative years. Together, Shtern writes in his dedication, they are meant to represent "the lives of Jews and non-Jews at the close of the 1920s." In Montreal the Talmud scholar and the Communist would not likely (or willingly) find themselves in the same room. At Mount Sinai they share a common affliction and stand on the common ground of the institution in which they are confined. Regarding the sanatorium as a "school" for the reader as much as for the impressionable young Velvl, Shtern's English translator sees the novel as "trying to evolve a synthesis of what on the surface are dissimilar 'weltanshaungen'" (1974, 13). In fact Shtern's main characters form a volatile mix of the political, religious, and literary claims competing for the loyalty of the Canadian (and American) Jewish immigrant. The voices that speak through Shtern's poetry are more often dissonant than in concord, but they are all *Shtern's* voices, joined in a psychomachia for possession of the Jewish soul.

Among the chief contenders is the "fiery communist" Itzik Truchansky who, appropriately, has "big red blotches" on his skin. With the *Freiheit* as his holy scripture, he believes that "the working class, soon or late, / will raise the hungry masses from the dust, / will put an end to war and wickedness and hate." He warns that

> Nothing will help the writers
> in the Jewish bourgeois press
> who spin their lies about the Soviets.
> The FREIHEIT is correct in its agitation
> that only Socialism will unlock the door
> on all the borders of the nations. (Shtern 1974, 41)

Where Truchansky finds his truth in the communist newspaper—including the truth that in a socialist world without borders, the Jew will be at home everywhere—Reb Shmuel pores over the Gemora, seeking "to comprehend the meaning / of a pious Jew's travail / amidst the mountains of a foreign soil" (40). To him, "the words of the Gemora / are still as fresh as water from a spring" (51). Even though he has been in Canada thirty years, he apparently refuses to speak anything but Yiddish, and he insists that "The alien tongue is but a sweetened poison / to open wide the gateways to conversion" (50). Truchansky's faith in radical "agitation" is set against Reb Shmuel's conviction that "God disposes," such that all things are "written, sealed and preordained" in heaven (53). And yet in Truchansky's political theology, is the ultimate victory of international socialism not similarly preordained? Reb Shmuel reminds Velvl of his own father, who believes that "German-Russ 'Enlightenment' / has terribly bewildered the thinking of our youth," and who "never loses hope / in the coming of Moshiach." In the end Truchansky fails to drive "off the apparition of death, / as his lacerated lungs / fight unceasingly for breath" (41).

From the perspective of 1967, Truchansky's death—the final, exhausting failure of his unceasing fight—presages the exhaustion of the revolutionary spirit among the Jewish party faithful in Shtern's circle after the Stalinist purges of the 1930s, the Soviet non-aggression pact with Hitler, and especially after the "night of the murdered poets" that saw the execution of Yiddish writers Peretz Markish, David Bergelson, Itzik Feffer, David Hofstein, and Leib Kvitko in August 1952. Truchansky's unshakeable faith in the messianic promise of socialism for the Jews mirrors Reb Shmuel's mistaken conviction that

> God's ways are just and straight.
> He protects his people trembling
> in the grasp of greedy tyrants.
> The wicked Hitler is not for long.
> Like all our enemies he'll soon be gone. (178–79)

If there is a "synthesis" of these two opposed *Weltanshaungen*, Truchansky's and Reb Shmuel's, it is to be found in the tragic irony of their predictions. For them, in the retrospect of history, the sanatorium figures as the repository of moribund political and religious ideals.

A Question of Language

If neither Moses nor Marx can lead the Jews out of the wilderness after Hitler and Stalin, what other voices from Mount Sinai can still be heard? Can the Jewish writer now forge the bond of a distinctively "Jewish" identity in the new diaspora, and after the failure of other prophets? Or can Jews "unlock the door" of their exclusivity (and their exclusion) by defining themselves in relation to the ambient culture? The former question engages Shtern's Mount Sinai patients in a debate reminiscent of what Italian Renaissance humanism called the *questione della lingua*: to what extent can a people's cultural or national integrity be secured by a consensus around language? Dr. Bond, though we are told he is from a Polish shtetl, boasts that his "birthplace is Berlin, / home of all the intellectuals." He "rants" at Velvl:

> Why do you compose your poems
> for the Yiddish immigrant,
> who's nothing but an ignorant churl?
> As soon as the ship sails
> into Halifax port,
> the immigrant, in sight of land,
> should toss into the sea
> all his old-country *jargon*. (Shtern 1974, 32)[5]

Insisting as Dr. Bond does on discipline above all, and given that he likes to parade through the wards in trousers "Freshly-pressed and tight —— / all in German military style" (32), it seems fitting that

5. In his journals, Shtern's brother Yaakov Zipper, the principal of the Jewish Peretz School in Montreal, finds the same attitude reflected in some parents who, having "received a taste of a higher social status," are "ashamed of Yiddish" and concerned that in a Yiddish school "their children won't make the right friends" (58).

he should be the secret beloved of the authoritarian superintendent Mrs. Glynn, who thinks that "everyone who's 'green' / is undoubtedly a communist / who undermines the good old days" (60). Dr. Bond's wardrobe choices hint that the enlightened Jew who would make Berlin his intellectual "home" adopts the language of his exterminators. Even if Dr. Bond means to say that Velvl should compose his poems in English, the implication remains that the immigrant who denies his Yiddish origins loses more than a language when he throws his "jargon" overboard.

The opposition between the secularist Truchansky and the pious Reb Shmuel is replayed in the arena of the politics of language in the opposition between the enlightened Dr. Bond and the Hebraist Meyer Glusman. Bond and Glusman share a prejudice against Yiddish. But where Bond imagines a world where Jews can unlock the door to a new home if they learn to speak its language, Glusman—once "the keenest student / in the shtetl House of Study" and for "many years a scholar held in high esteem" until "the white disease burned up all his dreams"—is intent upon preserving Hebrew as the definitive, and defining, language of the Jews. But not for all Jews, evidently, since he "boasts he hates the masses, / and therefore writes his poems / in the beautiful Hebrew language" (39). Although Truchansky parrots the slogans of the *Freiheit* and Glusman "speaks deliberately, with Bible texts" (39), they both share the apoplectic temperament of the zealot. For the "big red blotches" of the "fiery" Communist, the Biblical scholar is given a "fearsome glare," "thick red hair," and "protruding veins" on his neck (38). When he speaks, "Vitriol drips / from his lips" (39). The two of them are burning up with fever and burnt up by anger in the heat of their obsessions (the Yiddish word *farbrent* allows for both meanings). The language that Jews speak *as Jews* can thus never be disentangled either from the strands of their own intermural debates or from their relations with the politics and culture of non-Jews.

Even within—especially within—the narrower concerns of Yiddish letters, these debates are lubricated with vitriol. Truchansky is moved only by "fighting words," poetry that "leads mankind / to freedom's heights." He dismisses Velvl as merely a "pious poet." Velvl enters the fray but "secretly deplores the fact / that Jewish writers stand opposed / like vengeful, mortal foes" (42). To relieve the tension, Velvl urges his argumentative tablemates turn to another strain of Yiddish poetry:

> Let's read the poems of our Mani Leyb ——
> they're pure as music.
> Let's put our enmity aside and read the lines of Leivick
> those rapier lightning-strokes;
> his heart is torn by sorrow,
> yet he dreams of bright tomorrows.
> And the songs of Moise Leyb [Halpern] ——
> bold, tumultuous spirit ——
> a clear resounding horn,
> trumpeting pain and wrathful scorn. (43)

All three poets on Velvl's proposed reading list are associated in one phase of their career with *Di Yunge* ("The Young"), an aestheticist movement founded early in the century on the view that the soul of Yiddish poetry lay in the "pure" music and imagery of the language rather than in political posturing. Mani Leyb's 1914 *Shtiller, shtiller* (Still, stiller) "admonishes its readers not to shout in the bombastic tones of the Labor poets but rather to seek redemption in the quiet of age-old Jewish messianic hopes" (Chametzky et al. 2001, 217). Not by coincidence, two of Velvl's three poets were tubercular. Shtern will have known Leivick's "Ballad of the Denver Sanatorium"—the poet's "sorrow" followed by "dreams of bright tomorrows" touches on the pathetic and visionary strain of Leivick's "Ballad." Leivick would be the poet to read in the sanatorium. The invocation of his predecessor implies Shtern's commitment to follow in the footsteps of the ecumenical Denver lunger-poet who shows us how to put aside all the corrosive "enmity" that eats away at Velvl's fellow patients. From 1932 to 1934 Mani Leyb was a patient in the Deborah Sanatorium in New Jersey. Having published nothing for the previous five years, Leyb rediscovered his muse in the institution, where he wrote sonnets, a play, and perhaps his most famous lyric *ikh bin . . .* (I am . . .):

> We sang, and the echoing world resounded.
> From pole to pole chained hearts were hurled,
> While we gagged on hunger, our sick chests pounded:
> More than one of us left this world. (ll 37–40, in Chametzky et al. 2001, 220; trans. John Hollander)

The poet's song may echo through the world, as indeed it might in the day when Yiddish enjoyed an international readership, but it cannot cure sick chests, nor (despite Truchansky's insistence that "A Jewish poet must abhor / the men who fasten chains upon the poor" [Shtern 1974, 134]) can it unchain hearts. If there is any aesthetic synthesis in *The White House*, it lies in no reconciliation among the "vengeful moral foes" of the Yiddish literary world, but rather in Shtern's ability to channel their voices into the novel, which in this sense comprises an anthology of the many strains of Yiddish poetry from prayer to nature poetry, from elegy to angry diatribe, to poems of love or quiet reflection.

Shtern's attempt to recapture the feverish climate of Yiddish cultural politics at the end of the 1920s must be viewed in retrospect. That *The White House* is written in Yiddish and not in Hebrew or German or English would seem to settle the question of language debated in the novel. The assimilationist Dr. Bond would be surprised to learn that even in Canada an immigrant's jargon could still produce a work of literary importance after forty years, although he would applaud Shtern's decision to have the work translated into English. By 1967 plans were under way to establish the Leyvik house in Tel Aviv as a center for Yiddish writers and journalists (it opened in 1970). The YIVO Institute for Jewish research, founded in Vilna in 1925, had eluded the Nazis and relocated to New York in 1940. In 1967 Uriel Weinreich, the author of an influential *College Yiddish* textbook now in its sixth edition, was completing his *Modern English–Yiddish / Yiddish–English* Dictionary, published the following year under the auspices of YIVO. Weinreich's dictionary provided the "modern" Yiddish speaker with words for "mugger," "receptionist," and "telephone"—since supplemented in other, online, dictionaries with Yiddish coinages for "internet" and "link" (*farbindung*). The *Jewish Daily Forward*, first published in 1897, survives today as a weekly magazine in parallel English and Yiddish editions; only online does it remain a "daily." But by the sixties it was already clear that all such endeavors were, in effect, rear-guard actions intended to shore up and preserve (for scholarly study) a language that was losing its community of speakers. Once the lingua franca of Eastern European Jewry, Yiddish was now decimated by the Holocaust, fading in the diaspora with the passing of the first generation of immigrant speakers, and increasingly confined to pockets of the ultra-religious whose members had little interest in poetry. In the United States Isaac Bashevis Singer's wider reputation as a Yiddish writer survived and grew only when his work began to appear in English translation. During the 1920s, and with increasing urgency after the rise of Hitler, the Jewish territorial movement sought to establish an autonomous Yiddish-speaking homeland—in Africa, in South America, Australia, anywhere—for the beleaguered Jews of Eastern Europe. These efforts of course came to naught. In 1948 the Jewish homeland was established elsewhere, and its language was "modern" Hebrew.

The French Connection

In 1927 a creative work set in a tuberculosis sanatorium and written in Yiddish would likely have found readers on both sides of the ocean. In 1967, we have noted, Shtern's response to the likelihood of a much diminished, Yiddish-reading coterie was to sponsor the translation of *The White House* into the Hebrew, English, and French editions that would appear over the next ten years. Of these three linguistic border crossings, the French connection carries the greatest cultural significance. Along with its English counterpart, the French version of *The White House* (published under the title *Velvl*) would stake a claim for Shtern's novel as a contribution to Canadian literature and not merely a sectarian curiosity. In its publication history the novel's liaison between Yiddish and French reinforces the link established in the novel by way of Velvl's engagement with the French-speaking Québécois farmers in whose midst the Mount Sinai Sanatorium is located. In Leivick's poetry, as in lunger lit generally, the outside world is seen at a distance—through the window, outside the gate—as an inaccessible panorama of mountain peaks, sunlight, and snow, at once brilliant and alluring but unpopulated. Yehoash's evocation of the Native American past in his translation of *Hiawatha* may be based on some casual contact with local Indians, but Denver is nowhere near the fictional shores of Gitche Gumee. The area around the Mount Sinai Sanatorium, however, had been an isolated, almost exclusively French Catholic, enclave until the extension of the railroad to Sainte-Agathe-des-Monts in 1892 led to the growth of a small English Protestant community. Even so, in Velvl's 1920s, the people of Sainte-Agathe and its surrounding farmlands in the Laurentians were predominantly French speakers.

Velvl first encounters his French-Canadian neighbors on a walk through the woods, as he stops to watch the artist Goren painting a scene:

> A sun blazes
> In its cerulean vault.
> A house, a dog upon the threshold.
> A woman with a crowning head of gold.
> A tiny infant
> suckles at her pointed breast
> as from an ivory pitcher.
>
> A hunter with a deer across his shoulder.
> A barn. A raven rook.
> Amidst the rocks a bubbling brook. (Shtern 1974, 69–70)

It is not clear whether in picking out the details before him Velvl is looking at the scene itself or at the scene as it is represented in Goren's painting—an alluring, if arguably unintentional, ambiguity since it allows us to envision this woodland idyll, by way of Goren's canvas, as already aestheticized and sentimentalized. On another walk Velvl finds his way to the same farm—we later learn the farmer's name is Jacques Levesque (121)—where he is warmly received:

> Sacks of new potatoes
> smell of fresh-turned earth.
> The sky, red and iridescent.
> The farmer's wife, leaning on the fence,
> smiles affably and greets him with a blessing:
> 'Welcome, stranger!
> Here's a home, a door, a wooden bench.
> Traveler, rest a while
> You've covered many a mile.
>
> Have a drink of apple cider –
> cold as ice and we've got plenty
> You're new in this vicinity –
> stay over night.
> By candlelight
> you'll tell us of the city,
> where the reaches of the sky
> are strung with wires.
>
> The sunbrowned farmer
> his eye young and clear,
> offers him a glass of beer.
> [. . . .]
> With a twinkle of his bright-hot eyes,
> the farmer says: 'Come another day,
> I'll show you how we stack the hay!'
> The sun sets blazingly behind the hills.
> With a toss of her long red tresses,
> the woman says:
> 'I hate the rush and turmoil of the marketplace.
> Out here there's beauty, restfulness, and space.'
>
> She rocks upon her long and suntanned legs
> and laughs. (81)

The farmer's "sunbrowned" face and his wife's "long and suntanned legs"—on a later visit Velvl can't help noticing her "curvaceous, sturdy frame" (182) as the platform for her "pointed breast"—create an image of implausibly ruddy (and erotic) good health, in contrast to the pallor of Velvl's fellow patients, hours of heliotherapy notwithstanding. Madame Levesque is both the earth mother and the impossible object of desire. The woman whose infant drinks milk from her breast as from an "ivory pitcher" also "smiles maternally" at the young poet (182). If Mrs. Glynn is the wicked stepmother of the sanatorium, Madame Levesque is the nurturing natural mother of the woods. Sexuality, forbidden in the sanatorium, is here on luxuriant and unselfconscious display. Here, indeed, the stranger may feel welcome.

As well as a relief from the puritan discipline of the sanatorium, Levesque offers Velvl a respite from both the intramural bickering and the fear of death infecting the atmosphere at Mount Sinai, for the farmer and his neighbors are a generous and congenial lot. Levesque also offers Velvl a refuge: at the end the Levesques host the wedding banquet for Velvl and his new bride, a celebration to which everyone in the vicinity seems to have been invited, there to partake of an overabundant communal feast where "neighborly warmth" flows as freely as cold beer, appetizing juices, or mother's milk:

> Farmer neighbors, young and old,
> swallow massive mugs of beer
> and munch on juicy fresh tomatoes.
>
> Around the table bearing copious meat and drink,
> neighborly warmth flows
> in close and intimate talk.
>
> Fragrant steam curls upward
> from the roasting meat
> swimming in appetizing juices.
> Plates of pastry overflow.
> Frothy mugs of beer, ice-cold,
> from the stone-lined room below. (187–88)

This woodland fantasy satisfies multiple desires. The stranger in a strange land—the "wandering Jew" (70)—finds himself not only welcomed in, but honored by these warm-hearted and guileless people. The immigrant cut off from the shtetl comes upon its replica in this vaguely magical place, drawn by the warmth, the aromas of cooking, and by a feeling of "intimacy" reminiscent of the "My Mother's Shabbos" section of the *Noentkayt* collection. "A Prayer," from *Inderfri*, had dared to imagine a time "when Jewish farmers will cultivate their fields in peace" (1945, 112). The Levesques' farm provides a local habitation and a working model for the utopian idea, still current in Velvl's day, of resettling Jews in agrarian communes under the sponsorship of the Ad Olam movement or of such philanthropic organizations as the Hebrew Immigrant Aid Society. Like Shakespearean lovers returning to Athens after their midsummer night's dream, Velvl and his bride will return to "the city" nourished by the rare vision of a latter-day French-Canadian greenwood. As simple primitives, a tribe sprung from and still nourished by the Canadian soil despite their ancestors having been transplanted from Europe, these *fremde* who make Velvl their friend serve a similar purpose for Shtern as Longfellow's (and Zhitlovsky's) Indians serve for Yehoash. In this sense they represent an idealized mirror image of the *folk* the Jews could be if they were not cut off from simple, natural things and not bent on self-laceration. For Shtern's enfeebled Jews, the cure seems to lie outside the sanatorium, among a culturally, as well as physically, healthy people.

The White House, however, also offers a less idyllic picture of rural life in the Laurentians than Velvl's, or that of the painter Goren. It turns out that Mr. Breen, twenty years the manager of the sanatorium and himself a recovered lunger, confides in Velvl that he is now "working on a novel" about French Canadian farmers,

> a story which portrays Canadian
> village life as it really is.
> I think my stories of the local people,
> though they're published

in the Yiddish press of Montreal,
do have artistic merit, after all. (1974, 106–07)

Older and more worldly-wise than Velvl, Mr. Breen sees people like the Levesques through a less enchanted glass than does the impressionable young poet. Mr. Breen shares Velvl's empathy for the new Adam, a farmer "who cannot tolerate the city's ills, / its noisy streets, its tangled net of wires," and whose "most pleasant hours / are spent among the hills / or in the lowland gardens / that his hand has tilled" (107). But in Mr. Breen's novel of life "as it really is" among this disenfranchised and impoverished minority

you will meet
The toilworn farmhands.
In the mountains you will get to know
the poverty-ridden homes
of the simple, honest, French.

In his barn –
a horse, a cow or two.
From early dawn the farmer
wrestles with the
stone-studded skin of earth.

He must be made to understand
he need not be submissive, humble.
He needs a different way of life,
free of pain and want.
For from his piece of land,
his swift and skillful hands,
the only thing he has at forest's edge
is an old and leaning cottage. (107)

Someone, therefore, "must arise and sound aloud / the call of Freedom's horn" (107). If Velvl reads Mr. Breen's novel he will "realize it's long past time / to burn out poverty everywhere" (108). A snippet from the novel itself—Velvl has now taken up the manuscript, evidently—notes that "The Farmer-children leave / the clean and rocky land / and go to dirty jobs as factory hands" while their parents in "their mountain depths / . . . wait and wait for letters / from sons and daughters, / whose lonely footsteps are engulfed / by brawling city marts" (109). From this point of view, Levesque's people may be the last generation of farmers on the mountain. As we perhaps might foresee, the infant now suckling at Madame Levesque's ivory breast will one day abandon the hardscrabble life of her parents for a no less precarious factory job in Montreal. Life as it really is for these "toilworn farmhands" has become (in the current buzzword) unsustainable.

Mr. Breen's novel-in-progress within the novel thus serves as a counterpoise to Velvl's romanticized image of the Québécois as nature's children—a faux-nostalgic image in other contexts projected onto Native Americans (or onto the shtetl), Velvl's Québécois are a sturdy and hospitable race, admirable in their unsophisticated capacity to take delight in the simple pleasures. But Mr. Breen's disillusioned "hard primitivism" both corrects and complements Velvl's "soft" foray into the cultural anthropology of his French Canadian neighbors. Velvl's idealism only increases the distance between the farmers on the mountain and the Jewish lungers in Mount Sinai. He will never really be one with "them," however invigorating his interlude in their company. Mr. Breen's realism aims at closing the distance by political advocacy. His novel is intended to forge a bond between us and them by recognizing their poverty and by unveiling the underlying forces that uproot their children—to the ultimate benefit of the factory owner (in the Montreal garment industry, it must be admitted, often a Jew). As a source of cheap labor in the city, these Québécois children will stand (or fall) shoulder to shoulder with impoverished Jews in the "brawling city marts," while, in a trope familiar in immigrant literature, their parents in the (Laurentian) shtetl wait for a letter home.

Like the Jews, too, the Québécois were very much aware of their minority status in Canada, and equally concerned with the threat posed by assimilation to their survival as a culture and a religious community; and, like the Jewish agrarian visionaries, they "preached numerous campaigns for 'retour à la terre'" (Belanger). Mr. Breen's project goes beyond merely writing a novel: thereby, or by whatever other means, the French Canadian farmers must be "made to understand" that they, like the Jews, are the victims of oppression and economic exploitation, so that they will be prepared ideologically to hear "the call of Freedom's horn." But who will make them understand? Who better than the politically committed Jewish activist who would be their natural ally in the struggle. Of course the coincidence of these opposites lies in the fact that both "Velvl" the aesthete and "Mr. Breen" the political activist are the poet Sholem Shtern, who forty years later conjoins this double portrait of the Québécois in *The White House*.

More than any other aspect of Shtern's novel, the question of the Jews' relation to the French Canadians was, if anything, even more vexed in 1967 than in Velvl's day. By the sixties the debates between the Truchanskys and their opponents in Jewish political circles had lost their edge, the scourge of tuberculosis had largely disappeared, and—except on the *kibbutzim* of the Jewish state Velvl could not have foreseen—the Tolstoyan vision of the Jewish farmer plowing his field had proved chimerical. In this sense, *The White House* is a time capsule opened after forty years. But the prominence of the Québécois in Shtern's novel touches on an urgent contemporary issue. Canadian history records a deep strain of anti-Semitism in French Canada running back to the 1890s, reaching a peak in Velvl's day and after with the pronouncements of Father Lionel Groulx (1878–1967), the father of ultramontane nationalism, a fascist sympathizer, and a career anti-Semite. Anti-Semitism broke out in the 1960s with renewed virulence, exacerbated by the reaction among Jews to the growing, often violent, Jew-baiting agitation of the Separatist movement on the streets of Montreal.[6] Far from seeking any alliance in

6. These matters are documented in *None Is Too Many* (1983), by Abella and Troper, as regards Groulx's opposition to admitting Holocaust survivors to

their nationalist cause with the Jews as the other religious and linguistic minority in Quebec, separatists tended to regard the Jews as, or as a symbol of, their oppressors, and thus as a powerful faction allied against them along with the dominant Protestant regime. Father Groulx's movement celebrated the French Canadians as *pure loine*—"pure wool"—in their descent from the original settlers of the region, but as a race now degraded and lured away from their heritage by the influence of foreigners: the English and Americans, and not least the Jews, with their cosmopolitan ways and communist sympathies. Indeed, for Father Groulx, the French and not the Jews were "l'Israël des temps nouveaux choisi par Dieu pour être le suprême boulevard de la foi du Christ venu, l'épée et le bouclier de la justice catholique" [In our day the Israel chosen by God to be the way to Christian faith, the sword and buckler of Catholic justice]

Canada; by Belanger (1999); Anctil (1988); Brym and Lenton (1991); and most extensively by Delisle (1992). That Brym and Lenton's methods have been questioned (by Langlois [1992]) and Delisle's objectivity challenged (among others by Gérard Bouchard [2003]) in an ongoing scholarly debate underscores how fraught the issue remains. Longtime Montreal resident and YIVO archivist Chava Lapin, whose family was part of Shtern's circle of friends, recalls that in the sixties the city's Jews were terrified by openly Jew-baiting separatist rioters in the streets (interview with the author, November 8, 2012). As a result, Lapin believes that almost half of Montreal's Jews left the city for other parts of Canada—an exaggeration, but a telling one. In fact, census records indicate that from a high point of 112,020 in 1971, the Jewish population of Montreal fell to 92,970 in 2001 (Shahar 2003, 2) as many younger Jews in particular sought their fortune elsewhere. The decline would have been steeper save for the in-migration of French-speaking Jews from North Africa. Readers in the United States will be most familiar with the Quebec nationalist movement and the attendant issue of English-French bilingualism from the scathing (and hotly disputed) 1991 *New Yorker* article "Inside/Outside" by the Canadian novelist Mordecai Richler (included in his 1992 collection of essays *Oh Canada! Oh Quebec! Requiem for a Divided Country*). Painted as a fascist sympathizer and rabid ultra-nationalist by some, still revered by others, Father Groulx has an avenue and a metro station in Montreal named for him, although in recent years an effort has been underway to change the name of the station to honor the great (Black) jazz pianist Oscar Peterson, who grew up in the vicinity.

(1984, 393–94). True to his principles, Groulx believed that Canada should bar the door to Holocaust survivors. The publication of *The White House* in 1967 coincided with the year of Father Groulx's death, his passing commemorated by reverential obituaries in the Francophone press.

In this context, does the bond in the novel between Velvl and Levesque register some fond hope on Shtern's part of a rapprochement between these two peoples, despite everything? A cultural and political alliance founded on their shared minority status? A plea for fellow feeling at a time when Montreal's Jews seemed inclined to over-react to the anti-Semitic rhetoric of the nationalist movement by casting Father Groulx as the new Hitler? Perhaps, and yet, in "Jacob and Esau," a long poem near the end of *The White House*, the sight of the "hunter Bouchard"—his hair "thick and golden," his "hides upon his shoulder"—prompts Velvl to "imagine Jacob and his brother Esau / struggling in the dim and overgrown past" (Shtern 1974, 189). Shtern's Esau, the first-born son, believes he will "become the leader" of his tribe, "and Jacob, his brother, shall be destroyed." As the familiar story unfolds in Velvl's retelling, "Esau, tough and thick skinned, will exchange / his birthright for a bowl of lentils / and a chunk of bread," and Jacob will duly receive his father's blessing by the familiar deceit. But the story according to Velvl includes a detail not found in Scripture: Esau has grown "corrupt / and sacrifices daily to the idols of the heathen" (191). The "pious Bouchard" prays, but only that he might tie his "ropes around the hairy necks of beasts," and "strip their warm and valued hides" (193). At the end "Jacob flees from Esau's wrath" (193) as many Jews fled Montreal in the wake of the separatist movement. No mention is made in the poem of the reconciliation between Jacob and Esau as recounted in Genesis 33. In Velvl/Shtern's account, "Esau"—the Québécois hunter Bouchard—seems thick-headed as well as thick-skinned, brutish and hairy, more akin to the beasts he hunts than to other men. Although he came "first," he has lost his birthright to the land. Jacob "teaches all his sons" to "choose the God of Abraham / and He will lift you up / among the nations" (192).

If in the view of Father Groulx the French Canadians had supplanted the Jews as God's chosen people, Shtern now turns that story on its head and infuses it with his own small dose of venom. Shtern's French Canadians seem consigned to the same historical role as Yehoash's Indians—there first, but destined to be supplanted by a superior race of God's Englishmen. Remarkably, we are told that "Velvl talks to farmers of the Jacob-Esau days / in ancient Biblical tones" (193). He must suppose the farmers are unfamiliar with their own scripture and apparently too stupid to grasp his underlying point, if Velvl's conversation with the farmers runs along the same lines as his poem. Why, after portraying such a close and affectionate friendship between the Jew and the Québécois—implicitly, a response to the divisive racism of Father Groulx and his ilk—would Shtern himself end on so divisive a note? Perhaps his biographer, when one appears, will give us the answer. It is well known that there were direct and public expressions of anti-Semitism emanating from sectors of Quebec society in the 1930s and in the war years. David Shtern recalls that when his father "was working on [*The White House*] in the mid-1960's, the violent incidents set in motion by Quebec nationalists were very much on his mind" (email 8/27/13). Yet if in a broader sense the hunter Bouchard "with a deer across his shoulder" stands in for the brutality of human nature, then the countervailing idyll of the farmer Levesque offers the hope, or if not that at least the richly conceived fantasy, of a peaceable kingdom in which the Jew will at last feel at home.

Conclusion

FEW COMBATANTS in America's military wars before the middle of the twentieth century remain among us today. The same can be said of those Jews and non-Jews who fought the war against consumption under the banner of Hygeia from their beds in America's sanatoriums, and of those who provided their care, conducted medical research, and raised funds to fuel the campaign. "Victory" was achieved (against the "germ-ans") in the early 1950s with the deployment of the magic antibiotic bullet, against which the tubercle bacillus could muster no defense. Within a few years just before or after 1960, many sanatoriums became general hospitals, schools, or prisons, or were just allowed to fall into ruin. Like the disease that extinguished many lives and touched the lives of many more, the institution constructed to combat the ravages of tuberculosis was destined to fade from memory—or would have faded, had not the bacterium followed a predictable but at the time unforeseen evolutionary path by developing a resistance to all but the most potent pharmaceutical cocktails. When these, too, prove ineffective, tuberculosis will move beyond its current beachhead in the West among drug users and people with impaired immune systems and, as we are told, inmates in Russian prisons. It will more than probably invade the general population once more, free to thrive unless and until medical science can develop some new form of post-antibiotic of therapy. By working to recover the imaginary of the tuberculosis sanatorium, this book positions itself at a moment in the history of the disease between recollection and foreboding.

In my chapter on Sholem Shtern, I imagined *The White House*, a novel set in the late 1920s but written in the late 1960s, as a kind of autobiographical time capsule opened by the poet after forty years. It occurs to me now that a more suitably organic image for a retrospective study of Yiddish and the sanatorium might be that of a cyst. As surviving patients were told when they were discharged from the sanatorium, few individuals are actually ever "cured" of tuberculosis. Instead, most who managed to fight off the infection did so by developing enough immune resistance to encapsulate the pockets of bacteria that remained—and would always remain—in the body. Unlike other illnesses from which the afflicted recover completely, tuberculosis always leaves its somatic signature. Thus sanatorium alumni were cautioned to keep their strength up, eat heartily, and live quietly, since there was always the risk that stress could trigger a "breakdown." Survivors tended to speak of their lives "before" and "after" TB, and of their time in the sanatorium as a turning point more than an interruption.

The sanatorium persists as an indelible mark of the survivor's identity. As with plagues, wars, natural calamities, or the Holocaust, people who lived through tuberculosis carry the experience encysted in memory—and, if they are writers like Yehoash, Leivick, and Shtern, they carry it into their work as well. Florence Mulhern, author of *The Last Lamb on the Mountain*, began writing about her life in the sanatorium only years later because at the time TB "was hushed up, not spoken of."[1] The eruption of such memories is what we might otherwise regard as evidence of trauma; giving them literary form would both release and contain them. Although the lunger generation may have passed into history, the memories persist—bequeathed to children in spoken or unspoken ways, preserved in the

1. Author's interview with Mulhern, August 5, 2011. The scars of tuberculosis are emotional and physical. Over a period of a year, 1952–53, Mulhern was subjected to monthly "artificial pneumoperitoneum" treatments by which air was pumped into her abdominal cavity to collapse one or the other of her two afflicted lungs so it could "rest."

body of Yiddish literature produced by my three writers and by their unsung amateur companions in the sanatorium, and thus open to critical diagnosis. In the broader sense, this literature belongs to the genre of writing about AIDS, cancer, and the plague; in the narrower sense on which I focus, it belongs to the history of Yiddish poetry.

The tuberculosis sanatorium inducts its patients into a liminal realm on the threshold—Leivick's *shvel*—between life and death. In the end, either could be the outcome. If life, then the patient was granted a second birth, a second chance. The way down is the way up: vague but deep echoes connect this induction to a mythic descent into an underworld haunted by ghosts and populated by the living dead, as well as to a mythic ascent up the mountain—to the Colorado Rockies, or to Mount Sinai in the Canadian Laurentians. Survivor narratives tend to follow this arc. As Aeneas had encountered his father in Virgil's underworld, so Leivick raises the spirits of Spinoza, Heine, and Edelshtat, his ancestors in suffering, and Shtern, after forty years, revisits the realm of lungers long gone. Another root connects the American sanatorium to the history of nineteenth-century utopian communities founded on religious principles and devoted to healthful living, and still another to the leprosaria and plague hospitals of an earlier age. Both utopic and dystopic, the sanatorium as experienced by its residents was also uchronic: a place out of the normal time of their lives where intervals were measured in months and years of enforced inactivity. Bound by the discipline thought essential to the cure, the compliant patient would be an obedient student, an uncomplaining captive, and a willing (or unwilling) initiate into the celibate order of Hygeia. Love was forbidden as detrimental to the cure but recommended as a subject for poetry. Gluttony and writing were encouraged as therapeutic.

The landscape of sanatorium writing explored in this book is mountainous, sunlit, and snow-covered. Its background color is white: the "white snow-turbans" atop Yehoash's Rockies; Nathan Newman's "white pillow"; white snow, white sheets, a "white flame" in the limbs, "white grief," the approach of death from the "white stillness," all in *The White House*. Sanatorium writing inscribes its characters on this white surface and gives voice to the "stillness." Whether as the evidence of some primordial power of nature, or as the heights on which divine wisdom makes itself known—heights from which one can catch a glimpse of the Promised Land, or to which a father is directed to go in order to sacrifice his son—mountains tower over the tubercular imagination. Their sublimity, at once inspiring and terrifying, prompts an urge toward the sacred along more and less orthodox paths. Amidst the mountains Yehoash begins his translation of scripture into Yiddish and finds something deeply spiritual in his Yiddish *Hiawatha*, as Shtern does in his idealized Québécois farmers. Leivick's everyman Nathan Newman is no "Jesus dying, nailed to the cross, / Or Moses on the threshold of Canaan," and yet he is both, as the object of the poet's meditation on "life's holiness" and the mystery of death. An urge toward the sacred, however unorthodox and universalist, makes itself felt all the more strongly in these poets for their having been cut off from the world of their fathers—all teachers and scholars in the shtetl—and doubly exiled, first to the new world and then again to the land of the lungers. For them, the sanatorium figures as a faux-shtetl, the fragile replication of a community of Jews now bound together by their common illness if by nothing else. For Leivick, the poetry of the sanatorium addresses "a people far away, a people that remembers, as I remember, a heart and a mind that was purely Jewish." The "purely" Jewish, if there ever was such a thing, is now only a memory; and if in search of that purity memory wants to reclaim a lost shtetl-world such as that evoked in Leivick's poems on his mother's house, then it must, knowingly or not, conjure up a mirage that never was. For as Dan Miron has argued, the "literary image of the shtetl" as a colorful, warm-hearted village of pious Jews (in Sholem Aleichem's description of "Kasrilevke" for example, or one might add, in the shtetl of *Fiddler on the Roof*) is "an imaginary place, created by a modern Jewish writer" (1995, 1).

Thus displaced both geographically and spiritually, these poets face the central dilemma of the diaspora—the dilemma, not that of Jews alone, of preserving or redefining one's cultural identity on foreign soil, where inevitably one lives a hyphenated life. What does it mean to be a Jew? Need one even believe in the God of Abraham in order to qualify as the member of a "race" or "tribe" with a history and a book, but without a place? Shtern confronts this question most urgently in his depiction of a faux-community of Jews thrown together in Mount Sinai, sharing only their common affliction but otherwise at each other's throats. What could possibly bind the Marxist revolutionary, the assimilated Germanophile, the Hebraist, and the Talmud scholar into a cohesive *folk*? Inevitably for the poet, the question is bound up with the question of language, and particularly with the potential future of Yiddish not only as a literary medium or a vernacular tongue, but as the very ground of a "Jewish" identity. Should the use of Yiddish have an ethical and political responsibility as well as (or instead of) a purely aesthetic motive? Should it address local or universalist concerns when it speaks for the Jews? That everyone in these poems, including French Canadians, American Indians, and Henry Wadsworth Longfellow himself is given a Yiddish voice stakes a claim for the pliability of the language but not necessarily for its distinction as the mark of the Jew.

Perhaps the best phrase to describe this precarious identity is Leivick's. As we have seen, he calls the Yiddish poet a *fremde gest*, a "strange," "unfamiliar," or "foreign" guest—an "alien" not only in the new world or even in the old, but "on God's earth" (Harshav and Harshav 1986, 741). Never at home, always just on the threshold, he must depend upon the kindness of those to whom he is a stranger: "I knock, and I freeze; / I am frozen, good people, / Open please" (683). The tense relation between the Jew and his non-Jewish "host" is a staple of Yiddish fiction, and not just in the dilemma Sholem Aleichem's Tevye faces when his daughter runs off with a Christian. In *Der Khilef* (The Exchange), a story by "Mendele Mocher Seforim" ("Mendele the Book Seller," the pen name of Sholem Abramovich), an itinerant peddler finds himself stranded in the woods near the house of a "goy" after his wagon has broken down and his horse has died. At first the goy regards him with malice but in the end agrees to help. In return, "for the sake of peace," the Jew offers him the hide of his dead horse, so that "a goy should not be able to say that you shouldn't do the Jew any favors because he doesn't know how to be grateful" (4). By contrast, Sholem Shtern's depiction of Velvl's generous and hospitable Québécois neighbors poses a utopian alternative to Mendele's sardonic view of the Jew's engagement with the "other." Whatever the biographical kernel of the story, in Shtern's Canada the fantasy of a warm welcome for the Jew plays itself out only in the Laurentian greenworld of the poet's imagination. Like the Jews, the Québécois are a religious minority, tolerated when not despised. Unlike the Jews in the sanatorium down the road, they are brimming with health, harmonious in their enjoyment of life, and rooted to their simple way of life and to their soil, however rocky their outcropping of it may be. Embodying a kind of Tolstoyan ideal, these prelapsarian farmers are the mirror in which the Jew can see what he could be, or at least what he might have been—at home on God's earth.[2] In the end, these innocent children of nature, literary cousins of Yehoash's Indians, represent the image of a *folk* to which the feverish, bickering, deracinated tribe in the sanatorium could only aspire—assuming they would even wish to trade places with these mindlessly happy primitives.

Such questions of Jewish identity can, and have, been asked of twentieth-century Yiddish poetry with no reference to tuberculosis or to the sanatorium as the scene of writing. My aim in this book has

2. Among the many failed attempts to establish Jewish agricultural settlements after 1880, Cotopaxi, sponsored by the Hebrew Immigrant Aid Society of New York, was founded with a population of fifteen families in the mountains southwest of Colorado Springs, on a patch of barren land irrigated only by occasional and disastrous flash floods. A brief history of these doleful experiments in ten states ranging from Louisiana to Oregon is to be found in the 1906 *Jewish Encyclopedia*, "Agricultural Colonies in the United States," online at http://www.jewishencyclopedia.com/articles/909-agricultural-colonies-in-the-united-states#anchor4. In the same years, four agricultural colonies (one named after its founder, Baron Maurice de Hirsh) were also planted, but failed to take root, in the Northwest Territories of Canada.

been to contribute to the discussion by putting these questions into a sharper, if narrower, focus from two points of view, both converging on the sanatorium. Across time, a diachronic view locates each writer's lunger years as a crucial period in his life, and in his writing life—a period worthy of sustained attention as an index to a literary career. For Yehoash, the sanatorium is the prelude to the writer's career and the place in which his most ambitious projects are conceived. For Leivick, it interrupts the life of the writer at mid-career but turns out to be (so to speak) a period of feverish literary activity. Of the three careers, Sholem Shtern's most clearly underscores the lasting influence of the sanatorium, with the appearance of *The White House* after forty years of germination. My intention has been to fill in the gap left by accounts that treat these writers' sanatorium years as little more than a biographical coincidence. The Norton anthology of *Jewish American Literature* identifies Yehoash as a "poet and translator" who "resided in a Denver sanatorium from 1900 to 1909" (Chametzky et al. 2001, 139). The editors include the poem "Amid the Colorado Rockies" (140) and make mention the Yiddish *Hiawatha*) but not the dictionary or the Yiddish Bible, Yehoash's two major projects in these years. In the case of Leivick, a substantial headnote to the poems selected for Harshav and Harshav's anthology of *American Yiddish Poetry* says of the poet's years in the JCRS that he there "created some of his best, almost untranslatable poems, achieving a certain lucid serenity and writing, among other things, a beautiful sequel of 'Songs of Abelard to Heloise' and a cycle of poems on Spinoza. . . ." (1986, 676). Only two short examples are on offer: "Open Up, Gate" (737) and "Again a Neighbor Died" (739).

Looking over this last poem again, I am struck by the poet's moment of self-reflection as he acknowledges both the urgency and the difficulty of recording the event, as it were in real time: "And I am still writing [literally, "still writing *everything*"] with my pen, / Rhyming: room—gloom—doom" (739). Given this example, the reader of the Harshav anthology might wonder where the "lucid serenity" is to be found, and how the Abelard and Spinoza poems, not to mention the unmentioned masterwork of those years, the

"Ballad of Denver Sanatorium," might be taken together as a body of work with implications for Leivick's career before and after.

At the same time the synchronic view, developed most fully in chapter 2, establishes the local context of the Jewish sanatorium as the scene of writing. Attention to what might be called the lunger imaginary allows us to build up a "thick" description of the sanatorium experience. Taken together, the structure and practices of the institution, its ethos and pathos, the hopes and fears and fantasies of its inhabitants, the sense of place and community, the thematics of patient writing, all form a matrix that can be reconstructed in some detail from the archival records. As I have shown, Yehoash, Leivick, and Shtern all drew from and contributed to the cultural life of the sanatorium, whether by encouraging patient writing and sharing their own work, or, as also in the case of Shtern's autobiographical "Velvl," by entering the fray of literary debate. In short, the purpose of this book (I would encyst) has been to use the sanatorium as a key to the careers of the poets, and the poets as a key to the sanatorium. To the extent it may have succeeded, it will have made a contribution to the history of the sanatorium and to the history of Yiddish in the twentieth century.

APPENDIXES

WORKS CITED

INDEX

APPENDIX A

"Ballad of Denver Sanatorium"

H. LEIVICK[1]

[499]
It isn't Jesus dying, nailed to the cross,
Or Moses on the threshold of Canaan,
Just Nathan Newman—hear, I'll tell his loss,
On a simple bed by a simple wall.

And yet, in fact, there's nothing much to tell.
If every life were holy to other men,
The angel of death himself would then
See holiness in every human life.

But who holds human life sacred today,
The agony of blood and skin and bone?
These days how can you weave what legends say
Just from the death of somebody unknown?

The death of one, no hero or redeemer,
Somebody's death, the kind of man who'll go
To his rest, not in a covered sepulcher,
But in a plot beneath the Denver snow.

I say: life's holiness is not held in regard;
Worse—we grind it under foot: everyone

1. Page numbers correspond to the Yiddish text in *Ale Verk fun H. Leyvick*, vol. 1. 1940. New York: H. Leyvick yubiley-komitet, 499–512.

Who's able to join in takes part,
And who can't find a foot, a spear, a gun?

Still, my heart, don't give up your belief,
And let my song rise up in faith as well,
That he who is truly exalted shall,
In awe of the smallest limb, fall to his knees.

In fear he takes the other's fevered pulse
And temperature, and on his brow bestows
A kiss, falling himself in death's convulsions,
When the clock hand begins to speed its blows.

The hand of the clock begins to beat
With thunder from a live volcano rent:
A little tear—you can hardly catch it—
Boils like an ocean: violent, turbulent.

What is the din of cannon and of drums
Against the echo of two tired hands?—
And the dazzling flutter of waving flags
Against the shudder of a shirt collar?

He stands humbly by the sick man's bed
As silent as the field's last blade of grass;
He stands guilty and contorted,
Barely able to keep hold of the glass,

The glass of milk that Nathan Newman failed
To finish off before he left:
The little glass—not one drop spilled—
Runs out, now wasted, by itself.

But Nathan Newman—who is this Newman?
Why don't I tell you what and who he is?
Well—anyway, he won't be coming back again,
He won't be coming back here any more.

Anyway. A man like this. A Nathan
Newman. A dear boy with curly hair.
Sixteen years old when he came here, the man
Endured his hospital bed for fifteen years.

I could tell you things about his youth.
But nothing, in truth, that I can say
Will make him clearer to you than the fact
That on his bed for fifteen years he lay.

I would describe his body wasted thin,
And his clever face as well, but you will
Grasp his look if I simply say again,
That he lay here for fully fifteen years.

And in his fifteen years of lying in
His little room in Denver's hospital,
The world outside his threshold, down his steps,
Has gone through so much all in all.

[501]
Like thin candles, toward all the world's events
Nathan Newman stretched out his fingers:
And saw through their transparence, receiving
A white world-soul and a white meaning.

He still had a longing for his home town,
But with a smile and a quip he shrugged it off:
"A bed's the same wherever you go," he'd joke,
"And everywhere the same fever and cough."

Hidden in his heart he kept the lineage
Of martyrs, warriors—dream figures,
The bright image of an heroic age,
The vision of a clear, eternal truth.

But you see he was himself prepared
To step into that rank of valiant men:

Theirs was a suffering that Newman shared,
Marching in chains toward a new world with them.

Since he alone on his thin shoulders has
Already borne sorrow and need, the shame
Of oppression, the shame of hate, the shame
For those who have died of starvation.

Captivated, in his town, he would not
Stray far from the black prison door to walk
With the exiles even for a block
On their march to the eternal Siberia.

He was too young for prison chains,
But not too young to catch this deadly thing,
To wander from one hospital to the next,
Until he winds up here at Spivak House.

At Spivak when he came he was the youngest,
And in the course of time outstayed his peers:
His body—the lightest, the most refined—
Suffered through all those fifteen years.

[502]
Shackled to his bed, he would thrash from side
To side, consumed in desire, in burning dreams,
Until he felt that he was purified,
And to his silent walls said, "Yes."

In his yes, a number of things were implied:
I accept it. I smile at it. It's for the best.
The world is here. The room has four sides.
And the doctor says: The god of the world is rest.

The sun comes up just opposite the window,
The sun goes down just opposite the door:
The longest day and the shortest day go
Full circle around my walls and floor.

His yes also means: both pride and resignation,
And a complete break with the other side,
With those who keep on murdering the hours,
With those who continually lynch the time.

The song of time is first sung out in holiness
Here in the kingdom of tuberculosis:
Through flutes—the cellular web of lungs—
The thinnest seconds are breathed out in full.

The break is only with the world of bodies,
But not with the world of spirit born in dreams;
Those martyred in battle—he calls to them,
And look, he begins to stride, or so it seems.

He strides toward them. Whispers a word,
His hands embrace them with affection:
But no.—forbidden. He must, unheard,
A smiling mute, lie down again.

He smiles dumbly. It's good to smile that way.
A big world: a little closet with a lock.
A small table, and on it, two little books,
A thermometer, a pitcher and a glass.

[503]
A watch. A pen.—His faithful sister sent
Them to him as a gift.—
He writes her letters with a steady hand,
Takes pleasure in the firmness of his script.

He loves her. He caresses the dial,
And she loves him much, much more.
And one other is here. He takes a sheet,
And sorrowfully writes a trembling note.

Yes, there is another. But not a sister.
That is—a sister and something more;

He presses her last letter to his lips:
She loves him, and he loves her even more.

He writes: "It's been so long a wait for you to come,
And tomorrow you'll be getting on the train,
So I have taken up my pen in haste,
To let you know: Don't come to see me here again.

"Don't ever come to see me any more,
Not even just to bid me once adieu.
Tear my name out of your mouth, for I've
Already said to death: yes, take me too.

"Forget me. I order you. I decree it.
I clench my teeth. This doesn't mean I speak
To you in anger; on the contrary,
A gentleness sings in my bones.

"Because I love you I must cast aside
Every tie that binds you fast to me,
So I can then more quickly stride
To the goal that I so clearly see.

"At the Rockies' feet adorned with snow—
Such a small graveyard, a child's almost—
An earth clean and undisturbed,
A holiday earth, like a springtime leaf."

[504]
"I've wrestled with myself for years and years
To make this very choice in peace; and just
Now I accept it, not because I have become
Such a strong man, but because I must.

"To the very bottom I must go down,
To search the depths of suffering and pain,
I am sparing you from coming to escort me,
And, after, leaving me and going back again.

"You're young. The world will all be yours to have,
Go live, and take full measure of it then;
Meanwhile, greetings to you, with ardent love
From my pitcher, my watch, my glass, my pen."

Sealed. A ring. The nurse has come in.
"Please, send this letter off first thing today."
The nurse is always good to Nathan Newman;
She takes the letter and gets on her way.

"O wait a second!—Oh, no, no need to wait,
It's good as it is. Please, let it go."
The nurse is gone. From Newman's cracked throat
Onto the white pillow, the red begins to flow.

In answer to the bell the nurse is quick,
Returns to help, stanches the rush of blood.
He lies. His hands outspread. A hand—a stick!
But on his face, a warm smile rests.

"It's mailed?" he asks. "Of course," she answers him,
"But no more talk, my dear." And he obeys.
Suddenly everything begins to spin,
Swinging up and down, faster still it sways.

The swaying stops. He breathes more easily.
With sisterly concern she tucks him in.
She caresses his head with hot fingers.
Into his lungs he breathes the touch of her skin.

[505]
She goes out. In blessedness, he dreams.
He dreams—he sees a light in the wall, and
The light moves, dances and springs into flame;
And look: the veins of a human hand!

A man's hand?—Maybe his neighbor's hand,
From the other side of the wall,—the Yiddish poet?—

But how can the hand have crawled through the wall,
And here it is, already reaching to his bed?

A strange man, that neighbor, he won't lie still.
He hurls himself around as in a cell;
He carries the form of a song within,
And on a bloody threshold seeks to perfect it well.

The neighbor, visiting him yesterday,
Had talked of Heine's and Spinoza's pain
And death; isn't his hand now come to braid
All their deaths in a single wondrous chain?

Oh, it was good for him at last to realize,
That Heine lay for eight years in a pall,
And bravely fought not to shut his eyes,
Until the time he closed them after all.

And better still to hear, Spinoza too
Lay sick, and figured out death ought
To be itself a streaming forth,
The loving radiance of the divine thought.

And look,—a wondrous shiver: In Denver,
After all, lies Dovid Edelshtat!—
To be a third to Heine and Spinoza,
Has such an honor ever been man's lot?

He smiles again—at the impertinence,
(He falls back on the edge of the bed)
To compare oneself with the godlike Spinoza,
And to Heine the romantic poet.

[506]
But then a greeting, intimate and
Warm, from the face of Dovid Edelshtat.—
And now on the walls of the room, the hand
Again. The hand.—It inscribes a poem:

Oh, my good friends, when I shall die,
Carry the red flag to my grave,
The red flag with the colors bright,
Spattered with the blood of working men.

"Of course it's good to sing before you die,
But such, you see, is not my destiny:
My fate is that this Colorado earth
Through you, poet, should now belong to me.

"Oh, my good friends, when I shall die,
Carry the red flag to my grave too—"
And Newman suddenly feels a jolt in the skull
And the drumming chatter of tooth on tooth.

Now something gurgles up into his throat,
And Newman chokes it back, too weak to sing.—
Thus on a bright morning's broken note
Began Newman's last wandering.

The neighbor—I am he. The dying Newman
Captivated me, chained utterly
To his room. As soon as day would dawn,
I would listen for the footsteps of the nurse.

To hear her greeting, hardly waiting for
Her passing words: he is still here.
Her voice, ever attentive, tender,
Made the fateful sentence all too clear

In the early morn: the days are numbered,
And even the final hours perhaps are near:
Yet a wondrous, special strength would stream
Into Newman's body from somewhere.

[507]
It flows to him. He lifts his brow.
A glow plays on his lips, his whole

Face takes on a new wisdom, and now
A new breath comes into his lungs.

He lies and hears the noise the doors make,
And counts the rays of early morning light:
He wants only one thing: to stay awake,
Conscious—to be proud to the very end.

As soon as I cross his threshold, he
Feels it right away and says: hello,
And smiles: "Today I am a hero,
I've pushed the final hour back a step.

"Don't stop me from talking. It's good to start
To speak, at this moment to hear oneself;
I have to say goodbye, I must depart,
But maybe it's also good without farewells.

"There is something yet for me to grasp before I die:
To reconceive my body with my mind,
Marveling at the chatter of my teeth,
At the sprouting of the brow above my eye.

"Oh, who knows what a finger might denote!
How wonderful a fingernail might be,
How great a miracle a swallow in the throat:
And hear, how timeless is the crying of the feet!

"Strange that of all a person's limbs the feet
Are always cold, convulsed in tears,
Exhausted, they grow still more tired and weak—
Well, say, where shall I go from here?

"I would give up everything to have the power
To sit erect, if only for an hour,
So as to see death come, quiet and near,
And to say in peace: there is no death here.

[508]
"But what can I give away to anyone?
You know quite well the sum of my estate;
So I beg you—take my few little things
Back to your room today.

"The pen and the watch send to my sister. She
Won't see me any more—a pity, too.
Maybe it's good that way. Better maybe.
The book and the glass I leave to you.

"You no doubt think: see, he's trembling in fear.
I tell you no, and that you can believe.
Although the little crumbs are no less dear
That fall from the sated teeth of life to me.

"I'm tired. I'll fall asleep and dream. I'll rest.
I'll see my sister's mournful face—sad sight!
While you look through the window toward the west:
See how the Rockies glow in silver light."

He turns his own head to the window's light.
He sees the mountains. They have seen him too.
The Rockies with their heads raised white,
So close to the touch, they come to you.

The mountains gleam, adorned with bright snow:
Linked in brotherly chains, they stand erect,
Red wings hover over the peaks below,
And turn silver themselves, snow bedecked.

The highest peaks bend over, though, and bow,
Breaking the chain, or so it seems,
And start to span the valleys, striding now
Miles long on vast, primordial feet.

He falls asleep. I sit. I watch him go.
I take his whole being into myself.

Up, down, rumbles his breath,
Dashes itself, like a turbulent flow.

[509]
His body's in convulsions. All the walls shake
Like bursting dams. Torches of red fire
Are kindled in the window panes at break
Of day, and hurled in whirlwinds of desire.

The wind subsides. Drop by drop a cold sweat
Stains Newman's temples as he lies,
Two blue rings appear, sharply etched
Around the rims of Newman's dying eyes.

I sit. I watch. I am myself engulfed,
Myself dissolved into the mystery of suffering,
Of seeing the exhaltation of the lung
Through the open window into the sun.

I see it clearly with my own eyes: drawn in,
I myself become part of that breath,
As though the room were covered by a skin,
Stretched taut, and filled with burning, smoke, and death.

His breath sprays sparks. His breath flames,
Froth boils on his lips. His whole frame,
Lashed back and forth, rapt in a daze,
Like a branch in the woods begins to blaze.

Not just one branch. All the trees are ablaze,
The whole hospital is embraced in flame;
And I am there no more to sit and gaze:
Like him, I am a part of the fiery main.

And all the neighboring patients reel
In burning and torrential grief,
Singing their song to death revealed
With words restrained and brief.

And suddenly the peaks become the plain,
Under black smoke the Rockies smolder flat;
The flames go out. The crashing fades away,
The Rockies' fire dies down, and Newman's too.

[510]
And once again: he starts, almost sits up,
On Newman's face a smile begins to crack:
"Please, call the nurse, I'd like to have a wash
And put some fresh clothes on my back."

The nurse comes in: "Hello, my dear Newman."
She undresses him, washes his bony limbs;
She lays him on one side, turns him again,
And cleans his fingernails and teeth.

The sun pours in over stiff ribs
And thorny knees—the sun jumps back.
But the nurse's hands, like kissing lips,
Caress his limbs from head to foot.

She bathes him as a midwife bathes a child,
A newborn just emerged from mother's womb;
She puts him in a shirt fastened with bows,
And smoothes the bed white, freshening his room.

She lays him out, covers him with the sheet,
She puts a drink up to his lips,
And Newman jokes: "There once was a king
Who ruled a very, very, very long time."

The nurse begins to laugh; her finger warns
Him not to speak. She goes out. And he,
Cleaned, brightened, light-hearted,
Says: "Good neighbor, come here, please."

He stretches out his clenched hand to me,
In it he holds the watch and pen, I see:

"I have them ready, please take them away,
For something will surely happen today."

His was an expectant, holiday air,
But my knees buckled at the sight.
Not to take it would put him in despair,
And I pulled back my hand in fright.

[511]
But here his hand twisted, faltering,
And between his teeth he said: "I'll give it
To you tomorrow, ha, what do you say?
Let it lie here by me another day."

"Of course, of course," I said, forlorn,
"What's it mean? Let it lie longer than a day."
But my words only awakened his anger,
False comfort was all they could convey.

His eyes began to burn, and struck me
With their fury like a blow: "I am still
Proud enough not to have to beg for alms—
Another day donated to the ill.

"What do you mean—'longer'? what is this 'lie'?
Do you suppose it's hard for me to die?"
And all the words I thought might ease the sore
Have only served to rouse his pride the more.

But he came quickly to himself again,
And said, "Forgive me," mildly as a child:
"And, please, keep the memory that Newman
Did indeed preserve his pride before he died.

"I hope Spinoza won't be mad at me
For opening my heart to anger's lure;
Not everyone, before his death, can be
As great as he, but can be clean and pure.

"And now, do take these things from me,
Loosening myself from them now means a lot:
I can only close my eyes when I am free,
Not burdened with the smallest things I've got.

"And to her—my sister—say to her that I
Was given my bath by the nurse today,
That my hair was washed, as you have seen,
And that my teeth and nails were clean.

[512]
"And that I didn't suffer at my death,
But saw the sun with eyes clear and new
Just in the middle of the heavens,
And everything was white, and bright, and true."

I took the watch and pen when he was done,
And saw how a last breath is carried away—
While the watch hand runs and runs
And runs—into the radiant day.

Nine or ten men see the body cleansed. There,
By an open grave, nine or ten men stand.
A number on a piece of wood shows where
Newman will make his home, beneath this land.

In the neighborhood of Dovid Edelshtat,
In the same row, not far, ten steps away;
They have filled and covered Newman's plot,
And I myself was there that day.

There the eye is drawn to Edelshtat,
To his funereal monument of stone,
On whose granite face his own is cut,
And, as his testament, this poem:

"Oh, my good friends, when I shall die,
Carry the red flag to my grave,

The red flag with the colors bright,
Spattered with the blood of workers brave."

The people go. They leave it all behind,
The fresh grave and the old stone,
They return to the kingdom of fever
In the clear midday. And I, too, am gone.

A day of wonders—Who will see the like again?
Aside from the nine or ten with eyes so bright,
At the foot of Denver's Rocky Mountains,
No one has ever witnessed such a sight.

APPENDIX B

Archives Consulted

University of Colorado at Colorado Springs
  Kraemer Family Library
  Cragmor project Archives
  Newsletter of the Cragmor Sanatorium:
    Corn of the Rainbow (Abbreviated *CR*)
    Ninety Eight.Six, 1924–1932 (Abbreviated *NES*)

University of Denver Library, Special Collections: Beck Archives
    National Jewish Hospital Records
    Newsletters of the National Jewish Hospital:
    The Fluoroscope (Abbreviated *F*)
    News of the National, 1929–1943
  JCRS Sanatorium Records, Newsletters of the JCRS:
    Ear-Bender (Abbreviated *EB*)
    Hatikvah (Abbreviated *H*)
    The Sanatorium (Abbreviated *S*)
    Tales of the Tents

Denver Public Library, Western History/Genealogy Department
  Swedish Medical Center Archives
  Webb-Waring Institute Records, Papers of Dr. Gerald B. Webb

Pike's Peak Library District, Penrose Library, Colorado Springs, CO
  Glockner Sanatorium Archive

University of Washington Libraries
  PEP Magazine of Firland Sanatorium (Abbreviated *PEP*)

Works Cited

Abella, Irving, and Harold Troper. 1983. *None Is Too Many: Canada and the Jews of Europe, 1933–1948*. New York: Random House.

Abramovich, Sholem ("Mendele Mocher Seforim"). 2004. "Der Khilef" (The Exchange). http://yiddish.haifa.ac.il/Stories.html.

Abrams, Jeanne E. 2009. *Dr. Charles David Spivak: A Jewish Immigrant and the American Tuberculosis Movement*. Boulder: Univ. Press of Colorado.

Adams, A., and M. A. Poutanen. 2009. "Architecture, Religion, and Tuberculosis in Sainte-Agathe-Des-Monts, Quebec." *Sci Can* 32, no. 1: 1–19.

Alcott, Louisa May. 1983. *Little Women*. New York: Modern Library.

Anand, Geeta. 2013. "Global TB Fight Hits a Wall." *The Wall Street Journal* Weekend Edition (February 16–17).

Anctil, Pierre. 1988. *Le Devoir, les Juifs et l'Immigration: de Bourassa* à *Laurendeau*. Québec: Institut québécois de recherche sur la culture.

———. 2009. "Preserver L'Illisible: Presences De Sholem Stern Dans La Vie Litteraire Canadienne." *Archiveria* 67, 63–85.

Augustine, St. *Confessions*. 1998. Translated by Henry Chadwick. Oxford and New York: Oxford Univ. Press.

Belanger, Claude. 2012. "Ultramontane nationalism: 1840–1960." Accessed December 25. http://faculty.marianopolis.edu/c.belanger/quebec history/events/natpart3.htm.

Bewig, Mathew S. R. 2005. "Laboring in the 'Poisonous Gases': Consumption, Public Health, and the *Lochner* Court." *NYU Journal of Law & Liberty* 1: 476–95.

Board of Governors of the Glockner Training School for Nurses. *The Glockner Sanatorium: An Ideal Home for the Invalid. A Descriptive Booklet*. Colorado Springs, CO.

Bouchard, Gérard. 2003. *Les Deux Chanoines: Contradiction et Ambivalence Dans la Pensée de Lionel Groulx*. Montreal: Les éditions du Boréal.

Bryant, William Cullen. 1854. *Poems by William Cullen Bryant: Authorized Edition*. Dessau: Katz Brothers.

Brym, Robert J., and Rhonda L. Lenton. 1991. "The Distribution of Anti-Semitism in Canada in 1984." *The Canadian Journal of Sociology* 16, no. 1: 411–18.

Byron, Lord George. 1827. *The Works of Lord Byron*. Vol. 4. London: John Murray.

Caldwell, Mark. 1988. *The Last Crusade: The War on Consumption 1862–1954*. New York: Macmillan.

Chametzky, Jules, John Felstiner, Hilene Flanzbaum, and Kathryn Hellerstein, eds. 2001. *Jewish American Literature: A Norton Anthology*. New York: Norton.

Cooperman, Jehiel B., and Sarah H. Cooperman, eds. 1967. *America in Yiddish Poetry: An Anthology*. New York: Exposition Press.

Crapsey, Adelaide. 1915. *Verse*. Rochester, NY: The Manas Press.

———. 1977. *The Complete Poems and Collected Letters of Adelaide Crapsey*. Edited by Susan Sutton Smith. Albany: SUNY Press.

Dady, Ray E. "Ill Health and Thought." *Ninety Eight.Six* 51, no. 2: 1–4.

Davidson, Israel. 1911. "Hebrew and Yiddish: Two Parallel Forces in Jewish Culture." *The Jewish Quarterly Review, New Series* 2: 285–95.

Delisle, Esther. 1992. *Le Traître Et Le Juif: Lionel Groulx, Le Devoir Et Le Délire Du Nationalisme d'Extrême Droite Dans La Province De Québec, 1929–1939*. Montreal: L'Étincelle.

Derrida, Jacques. 1976. *Of Grammatology*. Translated by Gayatri Chakravorty Spivak. Baltimore: Johns Hopkins Univ. Press.

Dixon, Dorothy. "GRIT." *Ninety Eight.Six* 21, no. 1.

Dormandy, Thomas. 1999. *The White Death: A History of Tuberculosis*. New York: NYU Press.

Drake, Daniel. 1850. *A Systematic Treatise, Historical, Etiological, and Practical, on the Principal Diseases of the Interior Valley of North America*. Cincinnati: Winthrop B. Smith and Company. Quoted in Rothman 1994, 139.

Dworkin, Evlin Yehoash. *My Father Yehoash*. Quoted in Goldstick 1952, 11–15.

Edelshtat, Dovid. 1909. *Shriften (Writings).* London: Ferlag Arbeyter fraynd.

Ember, Aaron. 1912. "Review of Spivack and Yehoash's Yiddish Dictionary." *The American Journal of Philology* 33: 214–15.

Esposito, Roberto. 2008. *Bios: Biopolitics and Philosophy.* Translated by Timothy Campbell. Minneapolis: Univ. of Minnesota Press.

Foner, Philip S., ed. 1975. *American Labor Songs of the Nineteenth Century.* Urbana: Univ. of Illinois Press.

Forster, A. M., M.D. 1928. "Cragmor." *Ninety Eight.Six* 32, no. 4.

Genzlinger, Neil. 2011. "Things That Go Bump in the Night Don't Even Budge on TV." *New York Times*, September 6.

Gilman, Ernest B. 1989. "H. Leivick's 'Ballad of Denver Sanatorium': A Translation." *Rocky Mountain Jewish Historical Notes* (Summer/Fall): 1–9. Print.

Goldman, Emma. 1931. *Living My Life.* Vol. 1. New York: Knopf.

Goldstick, Isidore, ed. 1952. *Poems of Yehoash.* Montreal: Canadian Yehoash Committee.

Groulx, Lionel. 1984. *Lionel Groulx, Journal 1895–1911.* Vol. 1. Edited by Huot and Bergeron. Montréal: Presses de l'Université de Montréal.

Harkavy, Alexander. 1928. *Yiddish–English Dictionary.* 16th ed. New York: Hebrew Publishing Co.

Harry, Iza Duffus. 1881. *Between the Oceans; or Sketches of American Travel.* London: Hurst and Blackett, 101. Quoted in Ott 1996, 41.

Harshav, Benamin, and Barbara Harshav, eds. 1986. *American Yiddish Poetry.* Berkeley: Univ. of California Press.

———. 2006. *Sing Stranger: A Century of American Yiddish Poetry. A Historical Anthology.* Stanford: Stanford Univ. Press.

Hoff, Bob, and Lynn Gilfillan-Morton. 2005. *The History of Health Care in the Pikes Peak Region.* Bloomington, IN: AuthorHouse.

Holden, Harold, and Jack McManis, eds. 1947. *Poems by Samuel Greenberg: A Selection from the Manuscripts.* New York: Holt.

Horton, Philip. 1936. "The Greenberg Manuscript and Hart Crane's Poetry." *The Southern Review* (Summer): 148–59.

Howe, Irving, and Eliezer Greenberg, eds. 1972 [1969]. *A Treasury of Yiddish Poetry.* First Holt Paperback ed. New York: Holt, Rinehart and Winston.

Hunt, Ezra. 1883. "Hygiene and its Progress and its Legal Aims." *Public Health* 1:16.

Hunt, Rebecca A. 2005. *A Century of Caring: Swedish Medical Center 1905–2005*. Englewood, CO: Swedish Medical Center.

Kanfer, Stefan. 2006. *Stardust Lost: The Triumph, Tragedy, and Meshugas of the Yiddish Theater in America*. New York: Random House.

Katz, David, ed. 1988 [1928]. *Yiddish–English Dictionary*. By Alexander Harkavy. Reprint. New York: Schocken.

Knopf, S. Adolphus. 1919. "The Ideal Sanatorium, the Ideal Physician, the Ideal Patient." *New York Medical Journal*, October 18, 1919. Quoted in Caldwell 1988, 86.

Knox, Vicessimus. 1778. "On Novel Reading." *Essays Moral and Literary*. Accessed March 28, 2013. http://www.english.upenn.edu/~mgamer/Etexts/knox.html.

Kramer, Aaron, ed. 1989. *A Century of Yiddish Poetry*. New York: Cornwall Books.

L. T. B. 1930. "Something to do with Sex." *Ninety Eight.Six* 38, no. 3.

Langlois, Simon. 1992. "'The Distribution of Anti-Semitism in Canada': A Hasty and Erroneous Generalization by Brym and Lenton." *The Canadian Journal of Sociology* 17, no. 2: 175–78.

Lapin, Berl, trans. 1953. *William Shakespeare Sonnets (Yiddish)*. New York: Blokh.

Laughlin, James, ed. 1939. *Poems from the Greenberg Manuscripts: A Selection from the Work of Samuel B. Greenberg*. New York: New Directions.

Leivick, H. 1940. *Complete Works of H. Leivick (Yiddish)*, vol. 1. New York: H. Leyvick yubiley-komitet.

Longfellow, Henry Wadsworth. 1855. *The Song of Hiawatha*. Boston: Ticknor and Fields.

———. 1922 *The Complete Poetical Works*. Boston: Houghton Mifflin.

MacDonald, Betty. 1948. *The Plague and I*. Philadelphia: Lippincott.

Madison, Charles A. 1968. *Yiddish Literature: Its Scope and Major Writers*. New York: Frederick Unger.

Margolis, Rebecca. 2007. "Sholem Shtern: Bridging the Gaps." *New Readings of Yiddish Montreal / Traduire Le Montreal Yiddish*. Edited by Pierre Anctil et al. Ottawa: Univ. of Ottawa Press, 93–102.

McKay, Douglas R. 1983. *Asylum of the Gilded Pill: The Story of Cragmor Sanatorium*. Second Printing, 1990 ed. State Historical Society of Colorado.

Meltzer, L. 1922. "The Mount Sinai Sanatorium." *The Canadian Jewish Chronicle*, January 13.
Miron, Dan. 1995. "The Literary Image of the Shtetl." *Jewish Social Studies, New Series* 1, no. 3 (Spring): 1–43.
Mulhern, Florence. 2010. *The Last Lambs on the Mountain: A Story of Illness, Hope and Despair at Saranac Lake in the New York Adirondacks*. Victoria, BC, Canada: Trafford.
Murrell, William. 1920. "Fragments of a Broken Lyre: A Note on a Dead and Unpublished Poet With Ten Selected Poems Following." *The Plowshare* (January): 4–21.
O'Hara, Frank. 1971. *The Collected Poems of Frank O'Hara*. Edited by Donald Allen. Berkeley: Univ. of California Press.
Orlinsky, Harry M. 1941. "Yehoash's Yiddish Translation of the Bible." *Journal of Biblical Literature* 60: 172–77.
———. 1957. "Jewish Biblical Scholarship in America." *The Jewish Quarterly Review, New Series* 47: 345–53.
Ott, Katherine. 1996. *Fevered Lives: Tuberculosis in American Culture since 1870*. Cambridge: Harvard Univ. Press.
Parowski, Stephen A. 1930. "The Psychology of the Tuberculosis Patient." *Ninety Eight.Six* 45.
Radetsky, Ralph. 1935. "Patient in Denver Sanatorium World Famous as Playwright." *The Denver Post*, August 11.
Richler, Mordecai. 1991. "Inside/Outside." *The New Yorker*, September 23, 40–92.
———. 1992. *Oh Canada! Oh Quebec! Requiem for a Divided Country*. New York: Penguin.
Rosemont, Franklin. 1989. "An Introduction To the Poetry of Samuel Greenberg." *Arsenal/Surrealist Subversion* 4: 149–54.
Rosenfeld, Max. 1965. "Zhitlovsky: Philosopher of Jewish Secularism." *Jewish Currents*, June, 78–89. http://jewishcurrents.org/wp-content/uploads/2010/02/Zhitlovsky.pdf.
Rothman, Sheila M. 1994. *Living in the Shadow of Death: Tuberculosis and the Social Experience of Illness in American History*. New York: Basic Books.
Rubenstein, Rachel. 1910. *Members of the Tribe: Native America in the Jewish Imagination*. Detroit: Wayne State Univ. Press.

Ryan, Frank. 1992. *The Forgotten Plague: How the Battle Against Tuberculosis was Won – And Lost.* Boston: Little, Brown and Company.

Schauffler, Robert Haven, ed. 1925. *The Poetry Cure: A Pocket Medicine Chest of Verse.* New York: Dodd Mead & Co.

Seton School of Nursing. 1939. *Glockner's Golden Jubilee (1889–1939).*

Shahar, Charles. 2003. *2001 Census Analysis: The Jewish Community of Montreal.* CJA Federation / UIA Federations.

Shtern, Sholem. 1929. *Noentkayt: Linder (Nearness).* Toronto: Farlag oyfgang.

———. 1941. *Es Likhtikt (It Grows Light).* Montréal: Kulture komitet baym yidishn hilfs fareyn.

———. 1945. *Inderfri (Morning).* Montréal: Kanader Vokhnblat.

———. 1974. *The White House.* Translated by Max Rosenfeld. New York: Warbrooke.

———. 1982. *Shrayber vos ikh hob gekent: memuarem un esayn (Writers I Have Known: Memoirs and Essays).* Montreal: Adler Printing. Quoted in Margolis 2007, 95.

Simon, Marc. 1978. *Samuel Greenberg, Hart Crane and the Lost Manuscripts.* Atlantic Highlands, NJ: Humanities Press.

Staff. 1939. *History of the Glockner Hospital.* Colorado Springs, CO.

Stanford Encyclopedia of Philosophy: "Baruch Spinoza." http://plato.stanford.edu/entries/spinoza/#HumBei.

Taylor, Bayard. 1867. *Colorado: A Summer Trip. New York: G. B. Putnam and Sons.* Quoted in Rothman 1994, 141.

Thoreau, Henry David. 1906. *The Writings of Henry David Thoreau.* Edited Bradford Torrey. Vol. 4. Boston and New York: Houghton Mifflin Co. Quoted in Ott 1996, 13.

Trachtenberg, Alan. 2004. *Shades of Hiawatha: Stating Indians, Making Americans 1880–1930.* New York: Hill and Want.

Trudeau, Edward Livingston. 1916. *An Autobiography.* Garden City, NY: Doubleday Page. Quoted in Caldwell 1988, 48.

Waksman, Selman Abraham. 1966. *The Conquest of Tuberculosis.* Berkeley: Univ. of California Press.

Walker, Francis A. 1896. "Reflections on Immigration." *The Atlantic Monthly* 77 (June 1896), 822–29. Quoted in Trachtenberg 2004, 100.

Wallace, Sue. 1931. "Consolation." *PEP* 45, no. 1.

Webb, Gerald B., M.D. 1929. "The Role of the Physician in Literature." *Ninety Eight.Six* 37, no. 1 (May).

———. 1930. "The Prescription of Literature." *Transactions of the American Clinical and Climatological Association* 46: 262–79.

———. 1931. "The Prescription of Literature." *Ninety Eight.Six* 48, no. 4.

———. 1936. *Tuberculosis.* Edited by E. B. Krumbhaar. New York: Paul B. Hoeber.

Weinreich, Uriel, ed. 1968. *Modern English–Yiddish / Yiddish–English Dictionary (Yiddish).* New York: YIVO.

Winslow, C. E. A. 1920. *The Life of Hermann M. Biggs.* Philadelphia: Lea and Feinger.

Wisse, Ruth R. 1976. "Di Yunge and the Problem of Jewish Aestheticism." *Jewish Social Studies* 38: 265–76.

Yehoash (Solomon Bloomgarten). 1907. *Collected Poems (Yiddish).* New York: A. M. Yevalenko.

———. 1910. *The Song of Hiawatha (Yiddish).* New York: Yehoash Publication Society.

———. 1923. *The Feet of the Messenger.* Translated by Isaac Goldberg. Philadelphia: Jewish Publication Society of America.

———. 1926 [1911]. *Yiddish Dictionary (Yiddish).* New York: Farlag Veker, 2nd ed.

———. 1941. *Torah, Neviim, U-Khetuvim (Yiddish Bible).* New York: Yehoash Verlag Geselshaft.

Zdrodowski, Francis. 1949. "A Polish American Neoscholastic." *Polish American Studies* 6, no. 3/5: 60–86.

Zhitlovsky, Chaim. 1939. "What is Jewish Culture?" *Oifn Sheidveg (At the Crossroads):* August. Quoted in Rosenfeld 1965, 84.

Zipper, Yaakov. *The Journals of Yaakov Zipper, 1950–1982: The Struggle for Yiddishkeit.* Translated by Mervin Butovsky and Ode Garkinkle. Montreal: McGill-Queens Univ. Press, 1984.

Index

Italic page number denotes illustration.